Ethics and Librarianship

Ethics and Librarianship

ROBERT HAUPTMAN

Foreword by Peter Hernon

McFarland & Company, Inc., Publishers
Jefferson, North Carolina, and London

Library of Congress Cataloguing-in-Publication Data

Hauptman, Robert, 1941–
    Ethics and librarianship / Robert Hauptman; foreword by
Peter Hernon.
        p.   cm.
    Includes bibliographical references and index.
    ISBN 0-7864-1306-9 (softcover : 60# alkaline paper) ∞
    1. Librarians— Professional ethics.   2. Library science —
Moral and ethical aspects.   I. Title.
Z682.35.P75H39   2002
174'.9092 — dc21   2002000131

British Library cataloguing data are available

Cover art ©2002 Artville

Manufactured in the United States of America

McFarland & Company, Inc., Publishers
  Box 611, Jefferson, North Carolina 28640
    www.mcfarlandpub.com

For Dean John Berling and
Dean Kristi Tornquist,
with thanks

Contents

Foreword

by Peter Hernon

The question arises, "Do ethics and values truly matter?" Of course, the answer is "they absolutely do!" To me, in one sense, the answer is less important than the fact that people do not always act ethically. There are numerous stories of journalists, researchers, business people, government officials, and others operating in an unethical manner by falsifying data and stories. Whole articles and research studies have been fabricated, and the extent of research misconduct has not (and cannot) be fully determined. Nor can it be completely eliminated. Moreover, students may not realize what ethical behavior is; they may not realize that copying material without attribution and treating it as their own constitutes plagiarism. They may also neither realize nor care that the information they rely on is suspect or biased. Clearly, with the nature of publishing changing and with so much information at one's fingertips in a full-text form, information overload is, more than ever, a fact of life. How we deal with it has ethical implications and shapes scholarly communication.

The publishing industry today is seeing further consolidation, while simultaneously there are opportunities to create new visions about what comprises a "publication," especially electronic publication. In one respect, librarians are seeking remedies to the perceived high cost of publications (monographs and periodicals) and they are supporting ventures that may not be cheaper in either the short or long run. Understandably, they want to increase competition among publishers but, what is often forgotten, they must work within the framework of scholarly communication that exists within any given discipline. Clearly, technology and the digital environment will have an impact on scholarly communication; in fact, it is already doing so in some disciplines and fields of study. Librarians must approach scholarly communication from an ethical position, and honor that process in their own profession and other disciplines. To me, the central question becomes, "How do we honor and try to reshape that process in an ethical manner?"

Complicating matters, librarians are not merely, say, reference or technical service librarians. They are information managers who cope with the information life cycle.* Again, ethical issues and ethical conduct apply to information management. As the few examples given here illustrate, it is time for an extended treatment of ethics as librarianship enters the new millennium. Bob Hauptman touches on many issues, not all of which are simple to resolve (e.g., ones relating to censorship, privacy, and freedom of speech) and reminds us that we must approach complex issues in an ethical manner. Librarians could become an "ethics beacon" for others to follow. They must set standards and partner with other professionals to revitalize a commitment to (and interest in) ethics.

*See Candy Schwartz and Peter Hernon, *Records Management and the Library: Issues and Practices* (Norwood, NJ: Ablex Publishing Corp., 1993), pp. 197–200.

Preface

More than a decade has elapsed since the publication of my *Ethical Challenges in Librarianship* (1988), the first general, monographic commentary on acceptable practices in our profession. But surprisingly, very little has changed. Librarians and their progeny, information workers, are more conscious of ethical problems, and social pressures such as political correctness or Affirmative Action force them to choose carefully or adhere to certain regulations, but ethical consideration and commitment are still confused with legal sanctions, and people often make the wrong ethical choices, if they even bother to give any thought to whether a given action is ethically acceptable. This situation obtains in all areas of human interaction whether among professionals such as academics, doctors, lawyers, or hospital administrators, or for those who labor as plumbers, builders, or law enforcement officers. Sometimes the problem is blatant fraud or dishonesty, i.e., someone has made a choice to further an unethical or illegal agenda. More often, though, cases present difficult or unclear situations or in the worst possible scenarios, dilemmas that are really insoluble.

Librarians do not overly concern themselves with ethical necessities for three ostensible reasons. First, germane challenges do not appear with any degree of frequency. Second, the problems that do occasionally arise appear to be so insignificant that they hardly warrant much consideration. And third, because librarians work for organizations, they are under a contractual and legal obligation to act as the administrative representative (dean, director, CEO) decrees. And, naturally, the organization's counsel always has the last, threatening word. These are all false, merely convenient excuses to avoid taking responsibility for one's actions, speaking up if one believes that, for example, Affirmative Action or filtering, plagiary or petty pilfering are unacceptable, and acting in comport with one's ethical obligations both personal and professional. The disjunction between these two perspectives, for which mid-twentieth century theoretical conjecturing argued, has been a terrible disservice to our profession, allowing, indeed forcing, information workers to render service and provide information in an ethical vacuum. It is analogous to the case of a medical doctor who believes that abortion is murder but whose sole job is to provide contraceptive abortions to his or her patients. Most doctors in this situation would refuse to participate. Librarians are taught and enculturated to avoid consideration; their only task is to provide information regardless of consequences. When we do consider we create problems, although out of these altercations come new perspectives. At least today, we view unthinking information provision differently than in 1975. And Sandy Berman's revisionist work in cataloging has restructured the bibliographic record.

During the past two decades, we have seen a dramatic increase in the number of conference papers and journal articles dealing with ethics and librarianship. Surprisingly, though, there have only been a few books published on the subject; these include collections of case studies, an analysis of the ALA Code of Ethics, Tom Froehlich's (1977) survey, and some monographic treatments of information ethics, for example, Alfino and Pierce's (1997) work. But despite the major changes that have recently inundated our profession, no one has produced an updated and comprehensive overview of the ethics of librarianship. This is what I have attempted in *Ethics and Librarianship*. This new study is not a revised version of *Ethical Challenges*; it is a new work with new emphases. Some matters treated in the earlier volume are expunged here and other recent complications are carefully scrutinized in the present monograph. Taken together, the two books offer a complementary and complete overview of ethics and librarianship.

I offer my heartfelt thanks to colleagues, my students, and the percipient scholars who have discussed and analyzed various apposite situations. Without them, this would be a less useful work.

1

Libraries, Information, and Ethics

Libraries

The production, collection, storage, and retrieval of information has changed more in the last few decades than at any time since we switched from tablets to papyrus, from scrolls to codices, or from calligraphy to print. Despite the extraordinary alterations in what we do and the ways in which we accomplish things, libraries still exist in order to collect real and virtual materials that tender data and information to those who wish to learn or discover. Public, academic, and special collections continue to prosper because they provide materials, services, and environments that are unavailable elsewhere. Indeed, new services that mimic traditional libraries are now available or under development, including web sites or virtual collections that offer materials at no cost or for private subscription fees.

We live in an information rich society and there is room for many competing types of disseminators. Those that provide what the public requires will prosper; those that do not will atrophy. Traditional libraries may eventually be deemed superfluous. But there will always be those who prefer a physical trip to a real environment, where one finds real people with whom to interact and real books and periodicals to read.

Convenience and efficiency are only two of a host of important characteristics that help us to choose the precise course we follow in order to

3

acquire data and information. Supercomputers spewing out gigabytes of data and tens of thousands of electronic publications will never help individual students, researchers, and scientists to transmute all of this gibberish into real, useful knowledge. Mere physical collections will not accomplish this either, but their physical environment, so conducive to exploration, interaction, and learning, insists that the library is still a necessary social and pedagogical institution, worthy of public, academic, and industrial support.

With the development and evolution of information technology, everyone has become an information specialist. People now have access to the World Wide Web and its millions of home pages on every imaginable topic, as well as the additional resources made available through academic online public access catalogs (OPACs) and full-text data bases for searching and accessing journal literature (which any authenticated person may use), precise and sophisticated search engines such as Google or Yahoo! that help the novice home in on apposite material, along with excellently configured data bases such as "Expanded Academic Index" on *Infotrac* that allow anyone with a computer and a password to generate accurate results, or the bigger, broader systems such as the many Lexis-Nexis files that may offer a glut of sometimes inappropriate items, but that concomitantly allow anyone to do sophisticated legal research without the aid of an onerous education or a lawyer.

Anyone can find something on a topic, but this is really no different than the situation that prevailed 50 years ago, when a person could enter the research branch of the New York Public Library or Bizzell Memorial Library at the University of Oklahoma and locate pertinent books and periodical articles on the topic of his or her choice. Of course, a trip to New York or Norman was mandatory and the catalogs and indexes were more cumbersome to use, but the major difference between these two scenarios is convenience.

On the other hand, the results of the research are very different: in the past the materials were manageable, comprehensible, and with few exceptions valid. Today, when someone concludes a search he or she may have produced thousands of items, most of which are irrelevant, some of which may be in languages he or she does not understand such as Japanese or Polish, and all of which are of questionable validity. The integrity of web pages is especially dubious, and only those people who have learned how to evaluate this material stand a chance of acquiring reliable data and information. And it is here that librarians and professional information workers can be of invaluable service.

Information

Data and information are created, generated, articulated, published, and stored in various media; they are thus made available for consumption by students, researchers, and laypersons who either require anything on a given topic or something more exact, e.g., a specific piece of information, some previously collected data, or a precise article or web site. The naive, the unsophisticated, the untutored, and even many offspring of the electronic age are often at a loss when it comes to locating what they need, and since so much is available, they often settle for what they happen to stumble across. Sometimes, even a simple OPAC, a tool they have undoubtedly used since primary school, is confusing; they think that academic libraries in the 21st century continue to maintain card catalogs. People searching databases or websites on their own, with no help or guidance, may become frustrated with anomalous results or accept the first items to appear on a monitor.

Calling or contacting a public or academic reference librarian can help, sometimes dramatically. Requesting help from someone who is untutored in the subtleties of information searching and evaluation can compound the problem. For public and academic institutions to fail to provide these services is unconscionable; for information seekers to fail to avail themselves of these help lines is folly. Having too much (inappropriate) information is as bad as having too little. And knowing neither where to turn nor how to operate after spinning around and arbitrarily choosing is why, despite the glut of information that overwhelms us, so many are foundering in quicksand.

Ethics

All of our previous problems remain, but now we have managed to create almost insurmountable new obstacles for ourselves. Protecting confidentiality, avoiding conflicts of interests, affirming intellectual freedom and refusing to abet plagiary appear so much easier to deal with now that online pornography, copyright infringement, text and image manipulation, and filtering have reared their ornery heads. Legal scholars and the courts will continue for many years to sort out the new and difficult situations that have arisen in the electronic world. Nevertheless, the esoteric, legal, and technical difficulties that these possibilities present do not warrant abjuring our ethical responsibilities. For surprising as it may at first appear, virtually all of the new dilemmas presented by electronic informatics are soluble or at least negotiable within the ethical structures that have served us for more than two millennia. I continue to insist that merely because we approach informational materials digitally rather than analogically, we do not require a new ethical perspective; whatever is considered unacceptable in the real world is similarly forbidden in cyberspace. Vandalism, theft, stalking, abuse, rape, and murder are unethical and illegal evils regardless of the venue in which they occur. There may be some exceptions to this (hacktivism is a possibility), but these are infrequent and perhaps indefensible.

For thousands of years, an inordinately complex colloquy concerning the nature of ethical decision-making has been roiling the temples, the academies, and the scholarly and popular literature. This does not concern *what* is right or wrong but rather *how* one actually decides what is acceptable or not. But the astonishing fact is that despite all of the esoteric complexifying, all of the pedantic quibbling, all of the superfluous pilpul, ethical decisions are made in only two ways. Either one holds that something is good or evil and acts upon this belief or one considers the potential results of one's actions and acts accordingly. All of the extrapolations, variations, and confusingly disparate terminology, all of the disquisitions, tracts, studies, and adjurations from Aristotle to Spinoza, from Bonhoeffer to Frankel, are merely commentary.

Most people in most cultures at almost any chronological point in civilization's evolution have oriented their lives according to a series of principles, decrees, rules, or laws. These admonitory controls derive from and reflect the group's social necessities. Individuals are acculturated, trained, or frightened into accepting and affirming these tenets and they live accordingly. Those who refuse to cooperate are ostracized or punished. These general admonitions evolve into the specific beliefs and the belief system that the society's members affirm both intellectually or religiously and physically. Truly held principles or beliefs are the glue that binds members to the social matrix. Immanuel Kant (1949), in his *Fundamental Principles of the Metaphysics of Morals*, codified this into a precise ethical system, whose tenets are quickly noted. Those who act according to a preconceived necessity are called deontologists. They believe that it is wrong to kill or steal or prevaricate and they refuse to do these things despite any negative consequences. For example, although everyone takes pencils home from work or embezzles a few pennies now and again or picks up a television or small refrigerator from the rubble during a natural disaster, the deontologically oriented person refuses to capitulate. It is wrong to take something that does not belong to him and he simply will not, even if he may, even if there is no risk of any kind. Kant's four axioms provide excellent guidelines to the deontologically correct life:

- Always do your duty (i.e., act according to the controlling law or principles).
- Always act with a good will.
- Always act in such a way that whatever you do is universalizable.
- Never treat a person as a means but only as an end.

Kant gives no quarter: if something is wrong, it is wrong. The results of an action are of no interest, as long as one does precisely what one is expected to do. Only martyrs and lunatics are unmitigated deontologists. Belief is a strong master, but convenience is too seductive to ignore.

If one abjures principles and does not allow distracting beliefs or dogma (such as one should not commit treason for financial reward, murder defenseless babies for pleasure, or blow up airplanes for ideological revenge) to influence what one does, but rather acts only in relation to potential results, then one is a consequentialist. John Stuart Mill's Utilitarianism makes it clear that one can make ethical decisions by considering the effect that the action will have. Thus, taking a paper clip from one's place of employment and not returning it is so petty that it will have no untoward consequences. Therefore, although technically it is stealing (taking something that belongs to someone else without his or her permission), it simply does not matter. Taking two clips is also okay as is removing a few pieces of paper or a pen or even some hangers or small tools if one manufactures them and there are a superabundance of these products or if some are damaged or if a supervisor indicates that it is acceptable. But apparently books from a library or a bookstore, no matter how small they are, or chairs or computers or new Mercedes are off limits. Is this because these larger trespasses have greater financial consequences or is it because it is unpleasant to work in an environment where one cannot trust one's employees or peers? Since there are no principles involved here (e.g., stealing is wrong), the best the Utilitarian can do is to indicate that one should act in such a way that the most good is produced for the most people. But this will hardly do, since depriving Bill Gates of his fortune and dispensing it to lots of individuals and organizations would result in a greater good than allowing him to keep it. Pure Consequentialism quickly breaks down, as do the reasoning processes of those who advocate it.

The bottom line here is that very few people who bother to consider actions in an ethical context act solely as a deontologist or consequentialist. Most people do hold firmly to certain very specific inculcated beliefs, but they also consider the potential consequences; they then may manipulate their principles to fit the situation. This is what I call the ethic of convenience. Both a deontological and consequentialist perspective can help information specialists solve some of their pressing problems, but neither the unthinking application of principles nor the considered evaluation of potential results can offer easy solutions to tough or insoluble dilemmas. Because this is so, Richard Severson's (1997) approach is only applicable when the problem is clear and the solution obvious. Severson lays out four principles (respect for intellectual property, respect for privacy, fair representation, and nonmaleficence) (p. 17) that he insists can help information specialists make good, ethical decisions. But if all there were to differentiating the good from the bad path were a series of rhetorical queries or the application of some simplistic axioms, humankind would have solved all of its ethical problems in the late Bronze Age.

When a library director is faced with a fretful patron, parent, taxpayer, or law enforcement official who wants to filter or eliminate Internet access, because nakedness or gambling or cultural anomalies are offensive, applying a series of principles will not help, since the director believes that intellectual freedom and unmitigated access to information are the highest good. There is no room here for compromise, and it simply does not matter whether the position is trumpeted on the front page of the local gazette. Either all information is accessible, or whatever it is that a particular person, specialized sect, repressive government bureaucrat, or religious fanatic does not like will be expunged from libraries, the World Wide Web, books, periodicals, movies, museums, and so on. In this case the choice is simple: either we promote democratic principles (no matter how hard this may be to do) and allow things that some of us find offensive or even reprehensible to flourish, or we censor what we do not condone and create a repressive environment that forces those who differ physically, religiously, or intellectually from both the norm as well as from the fully empowered to suffer, hide, or foment revolution. We must be certain to avoid the establishment of any official or fringe group of vigilantes whose task it is to control the way we act and think. The secret police in the former East Germany, the cultural revolutionaries in China, and the Taliban in Afghanistan are examples of the antithesis of American democracy.

Ethical Confusion

We often know what we should do, but choose not to do it, or we do not know what to do and may consult a colleague, a director, or an ethicist. Since the stakes are not very high here, we often just do something and hope for the best. In medical research, if we transfer embryonic cells to a Parkinson's patient, improve his condition, and earn fame and remuneration, we may concomitantly be jailed for murder, so consulting an ethicist is not merely an option, it is of paramount importance. In the theoretical and applied information fields, most people already are aware that introducing a virus into the data stream and crashing millions of computers around the world is unacceptable behavior, but some folks do not really care, especially since this can be done anonymously.

And if we are faced with a dilemma (should one help a prosperous or seedy or foul-mouthed adolescent locate bomb construction sites on the Internet), we do not call upon Aristotle, the principal, or the Dean. We make a quick decision and act upon it. We generally do not consider requests such as this within an ethical context, so acculturated are we to providing help unthinkingly. Only when it comes to serving youngsters in media centers or public libraries do we balk, and here our hesitation is almost always predicated upon sexual matters. Neither the horrors presented in the news of the day or in the history of the Holocaust nor gratuitously violent video games or Hollywood extravaganzas deter us from coddling students in their assignments or desires. But as Inquisitors could not deal with blasphemy, so do many well-meaning 21st century people including parents, educators, and feminists find pornography to be intolerable. Concomitant violence is not merely acceptable, it is laudable, and that is why rugby, hunting, and fishing flourish. Parents take their very young and impressionable children to destructive monster truck rallies and psychopathic professional wrestling matches. These same folks want to filter the Internet!

Ethical Mandates and Compliance

Americans as well as foreigners who now live in the United States adhere to certain social and cultural tenets that are inculcated at home, in school, at work, and in society generally. Information workers labor under the additional burden of the socialization they undergo in their graduate work at both the master's and doctoral levels. Professionals in the information trades may have come up through librarianship, information or computer science, information systems, electronics, or even engineering. The perspective that the profession advocates is thrust upon the student at every turn, sometimes blatantly and sometimes covertly. The bottom line is that when the student completes an educational program, he or she knows precisely what the profession expects, what is considered acceptable behavior and what is unethical. Many job seekers believe that joining a professional organization will be beneficial and so they offer their dues to the American Library Association (ALA) or the American Society for Information Science (ASIS) or the Association for Computing Machinery (ACM) or innumerable other groups, virtually all of which have their own divergent codes of ethics that the new member may follow should he or she be so inclined.

And this is the insurmountable problem that continues to diminish the information specialties. All of these well-meaning adherents have created dicta and dogma, lists of suggestions and proscriptions, but only the medical, legal, and clerical organizations have any real power over their members and their right to practice. Information specialists do not have to join any organization and even if they do and are caught *flagrante delicto*, there is nothing that ALA or ASIS can do about it. With no way of enforcing their codes, the ruling members of these groups are powerless to castigate, to publish a list of transgressors, or to suggest that someone be sanctioned or fired. Not the least of their worries is the possibility of being sued for defamation.

Similarly, this is why the Modern Language Association (MLA) or American Historical Association (AHA) can do very little when a literary critic or historian plagiarizes his or her latest magnum opus. Scholars go round and round in circles accusing, denying, threatening — and often getting away with their crimes. Even in biomedicine, where there are mechanisms in place to punish fabricators, manipulators, or plagiarists, only a few perpetrators are caught, and their penalties, in light of their transgressions and the potential harm they can do, are minimal. Lawyers may be disbarred, but a researching oncologist may only be deprived of federal funds for a few years or may not serve as a peer reviewer for federal grants. For information providers, the codes and rules are in place, but not everyone chooses to follow them. The disgruntled, the dishonest, and the iconoclast risk very little. But this may not be as negative as it appears.

Noncompliance and Human Commitment

There can be no doubt that professional information workers do things that would be roundly condemned by all observers. They breach confidentiality, they violate copyright, they steal. (A high percentage of all theft in libraries is ascribable to employees, some of whom presumably are professionals. Occasionally, we learn of a library director who has stolen or vandalized his or her own materials for substantial monetary gain.) But since professional castigation is nonexistent here, the iconoclast, the person who sees things in a different light, is able to thrive, to

American Library Association
Code of Ethics

As members of the American Library Association, we recognize the importance of codifying and making known to the profession and to the general public the ethical principles that guide the work of librarians, other professionals providing information services, library trustees and library staffs.

Ethical dilemmas occur when values are in conflict. The American Library Association Code of Ethics states the values to which we are committed, and embodies the ethical responsibilities of the profession in this changing information environment.

We significantly influence or control the selection, organization, preservation, and dissemination of information. In a political system grounded in an informed citizenry, we are members of a profession explicitly committed to intellectual freedom and the freedom of access to information. We have a special obligation to ensure the free flow of information and ideas to present and future generations.

The principles of this Code are expressed in broad statements to guide ethical decision making. These statements provide a framework; they cannot and do not dictate conduct to cover particular situations.

I. We provide the highest level of service to all library users through appropriate and usefully organized resources; equitable service policies; equitable access; and accurate, unbiased and courteous responses to all requests.

II. We uphold the principles of intellectual freedom and resist all efforts to censor library resources.

III. We protect each library user's right to privacy and confidentiality with respect to information sought or received and resources consulted, borrowed, acquired or transmitted.

IV. We recognize and respect intellectual property rights.

V. We treat co-workers and other colleagues with respect, fairness and good faith, and advocate conditions of employment that safeguard the rights and welfare of all employees of our institutions.

VI. We do not advance private interests at the expense of library users, colleagues, or our employing institutions.

VII. We distinguish between our personal convictions and professional duties and do not allow our personal beliefs to interfere with fair representation of the aims of our institutions or the provision of access to their information resources.

VIII. We strive for excellence in the profession by maintaining and enhancing our own knowledge and skills, by encouraging the professional development of co-workers, and by fostering the aspirations of potential members of the profession.

further a new or different point of view and even gain adherents. An apposite example of this is the present author's perspective on the dichotomy between professional and personal beliefs. This bizarre situation exists in all professions, but it is remediable. (It must be intolerable for an ethical lawyer who may be forced to defend a guilty and remorseless serial killer, especially if the lawyer succeeds in winning the case on a technicality, thus freeing the criminal.) But doctors can refuse to perform abortions, lawyers can refuse to defend those whom they know to be guilty, even if found in contempt of court (though this flies in the face of our legal system), and librarians can make choices when faced with potentially harmful consequences, rather than merely reacting as if they were automatons.

Human beings owe a debt to society; they are expected to act in specific and acceptable ways. Sometimes these actions are so crucial and their breaches so detrimental that the expectations are codified into legal mandates. When these are broken, the guilty pay through monetary penalties, physical imprisonment, or both. Other considerations are ostensibly of less import and so they are not legally proscribed, but we must nevertheless avoid their commission, otherwise we are condemned for acting unethically. Sometimes the illegal and unethical jibe with each other, but not always. Indeed, they may conflict diametrically, as they did under the Nazis, for whom it was illegal to protect Jews, Roma, homosexuals, and the debilitated, all of whom were diligently murdered, after law abiding citizens turned them in to the police or Gestapo. Those Germans, Dutch, Hungarians, or Italians who helped, protected, and hid these people broke the law, at their great peril, but acted ethically.

Professionals have additional obligations. A harmless act in a doctor's personal life could have devastating consequences when performed in a professional context. A surgeon may mention her son's insignificant illness to his aunt or teacher in passing, but breaching confidentiality at work could result in a patient's suicide. It is for this reason — the many additional ethical obligations a professional owes— that there is an unbreachable dichotomy between one's private and personal beliefs. This is what allows the caring lawyer to defend the heinous barbarian, the kindly zoologist to torture chimpanzees, or the well-meaning biomedical researcher to detrimentally manipulate subjects who are in no position to understand nor refuse to sign consent forms.

This is why it is so crucial to understand that the ethical person does not allow professional obligations to his or her constituents to abrogate the more general human commitment that he or she makes by virtue of being a member of society. The received position demands that professional obligations take precedence over all other considerations. Stanley

Fish (1985) iconoclastically contravenes this absolutist perspective by insisting that whenever there is a clash between these putative obligations and what is normally taken to be correct or acceptable, the latter rather than former must take precedence. That is why the unequivocal separation of personal and professional commitments that information professionals advocate is so deleterious. When people dispense detrimental information unthinkingly, because that is what the job demands, they act irresponsibly. They cannot be called to task, because they are just following orders, so to speak. We have always known that this is unacceptable behavior, and the Nuremberg Trials confirmed this. German functionaries who "just followed orders" were subsequently executed. To act ethically is to consider basic principles, a course of action, and the potential results, and then to act in a responsible and accountable way. The ethical professional does not simply follow the mandates and fiats of the controlling organization or ethos, especially since the rules are sometimes formulated to protect the practitioner and not the client.

From Quills to Lasers

In the early days of American librarianship, collections were smaller, formats delimited, informational demands less frequent, and the general course of action socially, professionally, and ethically unambiguous. Etiquette, dress, and a calligraphic hand were more important than agonized discussions of acceptable behavior. In a casuistic environment people knew precisely what should be done and they presumably acted in concert with their peers. Public displays of iconoclastic behavior were not characteristic of the Victorian period even in the United States. As the years passed, education became a priority, literacy and the public library movement positively influenced each other, collections grew, and the needs of laypersons and scholars increased. Technology presented easy solutions to problems that librarians did not even know existed. We automated. Stamps, typewriters, photographic recorders, pneumatic communication systems, microfilm indexes on reader/printers, full-text journals in sealed cassettes, computerized circulation systems, OPACs, databases stored locally and nationally on mainframe computers with dumb terminals, CD-ROMs, and finally globalized Internet access to the known universe were all called upon to improve librarianship. And they have. But carried along with each innovation is some problematic baggage.

The precise implications of technological alterations are impossible to predict, and the ways in which we interact with new devices vary according to a host of sometimes inscrutable factors. Even a person whose ethical mandates are clearly formulated may be at a loss when faced with current contingencies. It is now possible to prolong life for years or even decades, although the infant's brain is non-functional or the centenarian is in a permanent coma. Even a person who respects life and is bound by unalterable principles must realize that this is cruel torture to those we respect and a waste of resources and money, and though ostensibly in accord with positive values, in reality it is an unethical and uncaring way to treat sentient creatures. This is a classic dilemma and for some there is no viable solution.

Technology often advances so quickly that social and ethical considerations lag far behind. We proceed by the seat of our pants, with some scholars, pedagogues, and administrators advocating absolutist dogma and others attempting (and often failing) to mediate between difficult positions. Technology has exacerbated ethical problems in the information professions so inordinately that social and legal structures that have served us for hundreds of years are being rethought. When tens of millions of youngsters download music using Napster, it is still theft, but even the copyright owners realize that something must change. Sony cannot have twelve year olds in Sri Lanka fined or arrested. The evolution, development, and commercialization of the Internet has even altered the ways in which serious scholars access data and information as well as the very standards and ethical strictures that control sociological research in cyberspace.

Understanding foundational structures and principles in addition to technological gadgetry and at least attempting to foresee where we are heading will help information workers to serve their constituencies in a productive, legal, and ethical manner. Medicine, law, and biological research are in ethical turmoil. Similarly, there is no reason why the information professions should be immune to new ethical quandaries produced by a dramatically evolving environment. Just a few years ago, the Internet consisted of email systems, chatrooms, bulletin boards, and gophers scrabbling around searching through unattractive data lists. Today we have a choice of efficient browsers and *hundreds* of search engines capable of locating precisely the attractive, graphic website needed. That it might advocate hate, pedophilia, terrorism, or other destructive possibilities that most decent, ethical, law abiding people find abhorrent, is why this book is necessary.

Solutions

Peers, clients, and society demand that professionals act in an ethically commendable manner. When someone's distant cousin turns to a life of crime, we may not be surprised, and it is possible that we expected no less. When a renowned heart surgeon, defense lawyer, or astronaut with a doctorate in neurobiology embezzles from the National Institutes of Health, defrauds a court, or fabricates data in an important experiment, we are truly shocked. We hold professionals to a higher standard and are commensurately more aggrieved when they disappoint us.

Sensitization to ethical theory, methods, applications, and expectations is crucial, if information professionals are to succeed and prosper in the heightened informational environment that we currently inhabit. The single most profitable way to ensure success is to incorporate serious and replete ethical training into the diverse educational curricula from which information workers develop. Many individual courses should have an ethics component, one that appears at different points during the quarter or semester. Additionally, one or two required classes on ethical issues should be part of all programs. Education in ethics is of extreme importance; students should not be led to believe that it occurs in their programs only as an afterthought in order to appease accreditation boards.

It is equally important for professionals to continue to consider information work in an ethical context. In-house discussions, workshops, conferences, and an ongoing familiarity with the scholarly literature can help to maintain currency. Sometimes, in the heat of our commitments, we may forget or ignore what is really important. It is very difficult to point out even flagrant ethical breaches to colleagues without incurring animosity. Furthermore, regulation should not devolve upon the shoulders of peers or administrators. Professionals regulate themselves.

If we are aware that some actions are acceptable and others flawed, if we realize that we do not always have the unequivocally correct path laid out before us, if we have managed to learn how to navigate the choppy and confusing waters, and if we care enough to try, then we will be better librarians able to serve our constituencies in a more judicious and equitable way.

2

Intellectual Freedom and the Control of Ideas

Cogito ergo sum.
— Descartes

Freedom of Thought

The pundits are wrong: we are not what we eat. The constituent products are transformed into glucose and we are assuredly not all sweet! We are rather what we think, and what we think derives from our perceptions. As the present author has frequently observed, there is always someone, somewhere, who wishes to control what we see, hear, touch, taste, or smell. Either the religious do not like Madonna or the self-righteous do not like Burroughs, parents do not like violence or the well-meaning do not like Neo-Nazis. The easy solution is to stifle their words and images, bowdlerize their books and videos, destroy their tracts and websites, and eliminate their discussions and rallies. As it happens I am not especially fond of Madonna, Burroughs, violence, or heinous political parties either, but I also dislike the barbarisms portrayed in serious films such as *Saving Private Ryan,* the rational arguments presented in favor of abortion as well as the religiously motivated harangues put forth to eliminate it, advertisements for alcohol and tobacco—especially when aimed at American adolescents and Third World children — or advocacy for the consumption of animal products such as unhealthful cheeseburgers or indulgent sable coats. But since I do not control matters, these things continue to prosper. Various religious, professional, political, private, or governmental representatives are not quite so tolerant. They are dedicated to the elimination of whatever it is they find abhorrent, unwholesome, or unacceptable. They do not like atheists, other religions, creationists, government regulation, lesbians, helmetless cyclists, or just about anything else one might imagine.

In politically or religiously repressive cultures, the demagogue, the clerics, the majority, or the empowered control what others do, where they go, what they read, view, or hear, how they dress, what they consume, whom they favor or marry, how many children they have, indeed, precisely what they believe. This is why the world contains hordes of unthinking people who believe exactly what their neighbors do. When one is intellectually manipulated and oppressed from birth, brainwashed to accept, believe, and unconditionally affirm a specific agenda, it requires a strength and perseverance most of us are incapable of mustering to counter it. After living in a controlled society where one misspoken word will result in torture and death, even a person who subsequently enjoys the rights and privileges of a true democracy may continue to whisper and look over his shoulder. Protective habits die hard.

Ideas Are Dangerous

Thinking is dangerous. It results in ideas, religions, inventions, processes, and revolutions, and most people prefer to stagnate. Naturally, devices that make life more tolerable or medicinals that cure horrific diseases are fine, but anything dramatically different, anything that rocks the precipitously balanced boat, is anathema. We are constantly embroiled in protecting the very things that least require our help: Gods, religious doctrines, and the inviolability of the state. Whenever someone approaches these sensitive issues from a new or different, i.e., offensive, angle, everyone rushes into aggressive posturing, court, or holy war. This may work in Albania, North Korea, or Afghanistan, but in a democracy it is unacceptable and, indeed, illegal. Not everyone agrees with the church, the current administration, or the etiology of dinosaur extinction.

In his introduction to *The Encyclopedia of Censorship*, Jonathon Green (1990) observes:

> All censorship, whether governmental or cultural, can be seen to spring from a single origin — fear. The belief that if the speech, book,

play, film, state secret or whatever is permitted free exposure, then the authorities will find themselves threatened to an extent that they cannot tolerate [p. vii].

Thus, it is no surprise that the most repressive governments censor inordinately. The South African Apartheid administration banned 18,000 books including what we would consider innocuous and excellent publications, e.g., Brecht's writings, Cleaver's *Soul on Ice*, Fanon's *Wretched of the Earth*, Heller's *Catch-22*, Hook's *From Hegel to Marx*, Miller's *Tropic of Cancer*, Nabokov's *Lolita*, and Rive's *African Songs* (Green, 1990, 290–292). Justice, fairness, sexuality, communism, and just about everything else seemed to petrify this minority government. It is equally predictable that puritanical societies will rely on censorious activity to cow people into intellectual conformity. Various American entities have banned influential books by Lee, Salinger, Steinbeck, and Vonnegut over and over again; and films banned in the United States include important and culturally influential works such as *And God Created Women, The Birth of a Nation, The Connection, Desire Under the Elms, The Exorcist, Lady Chatterley's Lover, Last Tango in Paris, Miss Julie, Native Son, Titicut Follies,* and *Woodstock* (Green, 1990, 332, 330–331). All such intellectual interdictions, in the United States and abroad, are unconscionable.

Indefensible Censorship: The Government

In a true democracy, the hard line is that <u>all</u> forms of intellectual control or censorship are unacceptable. There is only one exception. The First Amendment to the Constitution protects Americans from any governmental censorship. Neither federal, state, nor municipal governments, legislators, bureaucrats, or enforcement officials may control speech in its broadest interpreted forms. We are free to articulate anything we imagine. Sometimes free speech can cause others terrible harm, emotionally, psychologically, and physically. Thus, the well-meaning have passed laws, instituted regulations, and found in court decisions, all of which proscribe speech. <u>All</u> of these are unconstitutional. Many have been so ruled. Others have illegally controlled our lives, sometimes for centuries. Those who argue that racist speech, false speech, fighting speech, or pornographic speech causes harm and therefore must be outlawed are wrong. We have the Constitutional right to indicate our prejudices, lie about our fellow citizens, falsely alarm a theater audience, or describe our sexual perversities in vivid detail. The Constitution guarantees these articulations. Arguing that the founding fathers could not predict the development of

---

The First Amendment to the United States Constitution

"Congress shall make no law respecting an establishment of religion, or prohibiting the free exercise thereof, or abridging the freedom of speech, or of the press; or the right of the people peaceably to assemble, and to petition the Government for a redress of grievances."

---

mass media, cellular telephones, instantaneous global Internet communication, or just how perverse we would be is to superimpose technological and cultural change on a deontological principle. If we are to be organized, structured, and ruled by law (i.e., the Constitution) rather than by chaos or whim, we must abide by the law, even when the consequences are undesirable. This much must be patently clear to anyone who thinks this through theoretically, i.e., outside of a social context.

Problems only arise when we try to live with this absolute mandate in the real world. How can we unequivocally affirm the First Amendment and simultaneously protect minorities from racist claptrap, individuals from false accusations, groups from alarms that result in harmful action (e.g., trampling, in an attempt to escape from a non-existent emergency), or children from inappropriate material? The answer to this dilemma is really quite simple. The courts must allow the speech but punish the harmful result. If someone falsely claims that a senator or celebrity is guilty of embezzlement or adultery, then the individual involved would sue for libel or slander and collect damages. The state may criminalize the result, in this case the false accusation that causes harm, and prosecute as well. If someone articulates racist doctrine, that is his right. But if an individual or group can prove harm, then he would be liable or subject to prosecution depending on the context and consequences of the articulation, but not on the articulation itself. Similar cases can be made for all other forms of proscribed speech. This soft version of accountability should not be confused with the McKinnon/Dworkin initiative, which holds the primary person — the creator of sexually oriented depictions — responsible for harm perpetrated by a secondary individual — the abuser, the rapist, the serial killer — who ostensibly traces the etiology of the physical act back to the sexual depiction. In this case, the culpable party is whoever commits the atrocity and not the creator of the proximate cause. Is this mere pilpul? Will the results turn out to be the same?

I think not. Under this more just system, speech itself would not be regulated, and the government would no longer attempt to censor, e.g., sexually oriented materials. The only reasonable exception to all of this might be dangerously sensitive state secrets, e.g., the codes that launch nuclear missiles. If we fail to affirm our principles (even when we sincerely believe that decency and justice demand regulation), we will degenerate into totalitarianism. Then the Constitution will no longer matter.

Indefensible Censorship: The Public

If material manages to evade the government's interference, it still must pass muster with the public, all of the self-appointed individuals, committees, groups, leagues, organizations, and associations that arbitrarily or officially can importune, wheedle, complain, demand, threaten, boycott, sue, or otherwise influence group members, publishers, producers, television and radio stations, book and video stores, and librarians to avoid or expunge a particular item on any imaginable topic. An astonishing mid-century case involved a consortium of well-known scientists who pressured a publishing house to transfer *Worlds in Collision,* Immanuel Velikovsky's iconoclastic discussion of terrestrial change, to another publisher. The public's power to exert moral suasion or to influence the availability of material varies over time. During the Renaissance (when the church was a quasi-governmental organization), blasphemers were executed and Galileo was forced to recant a scientific theory. During the course of many years, John S. Sumner of the New York Society for the Prevention of Vice harassed Frances Steloff and dragged her into court. In 1946, he forced her to cover some innocuous anatomy in the Gotham Book Mart window (Rogers, 1965). Publicly displayed or articulated images of naked, blasphemous, violent, or other offensive or suggestive material stimulate the self-appointed into action. Tipper Gore managed to convince the recording industry to label its products so that children could be proscribed from purchasing some singer's vulgar rubbish.

Over the years, as Joan Kennedy Taylor (1997) observes, the censorious have targeted specific areas for special emphasis. Since the Supreme Court has curtailed censorship in relation to national security and the protection of women, the overly protective are now concentrating on children. But despite their successes, it is now more difficult for non-governmental individuals or groups to pressure commercial or public establishments into making alterations. For example, whereas Cincinnati did capitulate to the benighted and forced the Mapplethorpe show to close, the recent brouhaha at the Brooklyn Museum concerning Ofili's images had little effect on the display; all of the ranting merely attracted international attention to some otherwise shoddy art works. (Both of these cases also involved the government.) Performers at happenings and creators of shock art purposely offend in the most egregious fashion; they do things that are painfully repulsive in order to entertain the jaded. If this is too offensive for someone, he or she should not participate. Neither individuals nor those who have banded together into groups, in order to further a specific agenda, have the right to control the productions of others. But what is truly amazing is where the public draws its line. The most horrendous visual depictions of violence are perfectly acceptable to suburban parents, who send their bored adolescents off to slasher films, while they enjoy some serene moments at *Taxi Driver* or *Silence of the Lambs.* But let two anatomically divergent body parts come into contact with each other, mention Darwin, gay or lesbian love, or a predilection for Daoism, and these same folks rally to picket the theater or bar the speaker from the podium. Astonishingly, the same situation obtains in academia. Everyone is welcome on campus, which is, after all, the home of diverse opinion and investigation — except for the publisher of *Hustler,* creationists, scholarly commentators on IQ divergence, bigots, and any other offensive or iconoclastic thinker.

Censorship and Libraries

Public, academic, and special librarians select materials for their collections based on current and future need. No law library, whether affiliated with a university or housed in a large private firm, subscribes to *Seventeen, PMLA,* or *Nuclear Instrumentation,* at least not for professional purposes, nor does it purchase large numbers of romances, adventure videos, or rap CDs. The selection criteria at work here insist upon materials that are relevant to the practice of law (and any necessary ancillary area, e.g., the environment). This, as Lester Asheim (1953) pointed out a half century ago, is not censorship. No library can acquire everything and none, except perhaps a national library, would want to own all publications and media formats in all disciplinary areas. Both sexually explicit magazines as well as scholarly disquisitions on topology would be out of place in a children's collection. Despite the clarity and ubiquity of this explanation, people still confuse selection and censorship. The former allows a layperson to suggest or a professional to select appropriate items; the latter prescribes an *a priori* limitation on specific materials based on specious reasoning, religious or ideological persuasion, or emotional reaction.

All types of libraries are harmed by various forms of censorship including challenges, demands, threats, legal actions, vandalism, and theft. But it is the school media center, which sometimes serves a clientele consisting of both very young children as well as high school seniors (some of whom may be married and have children of their own), that bears the public's true wrath. The classroom suffers as well. As Robert S. Peck (1996) notes, in 1985, textbooks were censored more than 130 times in 44 states. In 1987, *The Diary of Anne Frank* and *The Wizard of Oz* were singled out as "anti–Christian" and the teaching of evolution was banned unless creationism was also given equal time in the classroom. The censors were eventually defeated but as Peck reminds us, incidents such as these chill the intellectual climate, and force people to hesitate before thinking in vibrant and unusual ways.

Students in librarianship are acculturated to defend intellectual freedom and abjure censorship. The general consensus seems to be that they accept this responsibility and that they continue to do so in the field. Yet, the 328 respondents who comprised Frances Beck McDonald's (1993) survey of Midwestern secondary school librarians indicated that although they agreed with intellectual freedom principles, they disagreed with their application. These "librarians were ... restrictive in all categories of potential censorship: policy, selection, access, and diversity" (p. 134). The problems media specialists face are so blatant and the immediate threats so daunting that even the caring, the judicious, and the defenders of free speech may capitulate.

Some years ago, in discussions held in a graduate selection course that I offered, many of the adult students, virtually all of whom were employed as media specialists, insisted that censorship was unacceptable and then went on to detail the many cases in which they were forced to remove materials from their libraries. One of the students solicited additional evidence from a listserv, and the class members contributed written documentation. I compiled and restructured this, which all 15 of us published as "Pragmatic Capitulation: Why the Information Specialist Censors" (Buesseler et al., 1999). The situations are predictable: we self-censor in selection, since we know that books, magazines, videos, and software that deal with sex, drugs, or rock-n-roll will elicit howls of protest; the self-righteous bombard us with demands to remove all offensive or taboo material from the shelves; and other employees carefully monitor the computer screens of their charges. What comes as a surprise is that administrative actions and threats are so unrelenting and that the professionals cannot bring themselves to fight back, despite the many court cases that affirm the rights of those who wish to pursue divergent inquiries in both primary and secondary school collections and classrooms. A principal removed a book and denied it; a librarian, under pressure, disposed of a volume; a principal cancelled the school's subscription to *Rolling Stone*

The Library Bill of Rights

The American Library Association affirms that all libraries are forums for information and ideas, and that the following basic policies should guide their services.

I. Books and other library resources should be provided for the interest, information, and enlightenment of all people of the community the library serves. Materials should not be excluded because of the origin, background, or views of those contributing to their creation.

II. Libraries should provide materials and information presenting all points of view on current and historical issues. Materials should not be proscribed or removed because of partisan or doctrinal disapproval.

III. Libraries should challenge censorship in the fulfillment of their responsibility to provide information and enlightenment.

IV. Libraries should cooperate with all persons and groups concerned with resisting abridgment of free expression and free access to ideas.

V. A person's right to use a library should not be denied or abridged because of origin, age, background, or views.

VI. Libraries which make exhibit spaces and meeting rooms available to the public they serve should make such facilities available on an equitable basis, regardless of the beliefs or affiliations of individuals or groups requesting their use.

Adopted June 18, 1948. Amended by the ALA Council February 2, 1961; June 27, 1967; and January 23, 1980; reaffirmed January 23, 1996.

during the librarians' vacation; and administrators indicated that if books on pregnancy, birth control, condoms or AIDS were shelved, the librarian would be fired.

No parent or cabal of parents, no principal, no board member, has the right to insist that a school deprive all of its students by eliminating *Catcher in the Rye, Daddy's Roommate,* or anything else from the curriculum or the media center collection. The Supreme Court's split but positive decision in *Board of Education Island Trees Union Free School District No. 26 v. Pico* (1982) set an important precedent for the protection of students' First Amendment rights. A diverse student body may not be coddled and protected from ideas, images, and articulations that displease those who tenaciously defend specific religious, political, or cultural agendas.

The same pressure may be brought to bear on public and academic librarians, but here, with the exception of children's materials, we are on surer ground. Large, diverse public collections are similar to college and university libraries. The New York Public's research divisions or the Carnegie Library in Pittsburgh select and acquire in all areas. Some public collections are as good as anything found in the academy; the theater materials at the New York Public, for example, are unsurpassed. But smaller public facilities, especially those serving a conservative clientele, do not have the resources to fight the never-ending demands. A precise policy and challenge procedure as well as solid knowledge of the materials covered in the *Intellectual Freedom Manual* (Office for Intellectual Freedom, 1996), especially the "Library Bill of Rights," may help, but mere documents cannot solve the general problem, viz., closed-minded intolerance, and only an expensive legal imbroglio may decide the specific issue. Once it is won, other books or videos or ideas will stimulate a second and then a third request to remove something offensive. It is a never-ending battle.

All academic collections, but especially those at research institutions, are generally immune to the attacks so typical at the primary and secondary school level. The university environment requires the collection of and access to materials in all areas of human endeavor, even those that are considered offensive, dangerous, repulsive, barbaric, or horrific. Only a Comstockian legislator or religious fanatic would wander the Harvard or Michigan stacks or online catalogue searching for unacceptable material, and then either rail against it in the Senate or popular press or destroy it in some way. As it happens, occurrences such as these do sometimes take place, but the libraries defend themselves, replace lost items, and continue to build their collections.

Electronic Censorship

Global electronic access has confused an already untenable situation. Patrons' ability to access and record copyrighted music through Napster bothers directors and deans far less than the probability that some student will access a site that caters to those who satisfy their sexual cravings virtually. These images are unacceptable to the puritanical, and administrators fear social, financial, and legal repercussions should another patron take offense at what appears on a neighboring screen. That the offended can stop snooping, turn away, or leave, that monitors can be shielded, that online academic research unsympathetic to pornography might entail its viewing are all obvious to those in control, but this does not stop them from imposing rules, requiring parental permission, demanding pledges, or installing filtering software. These procedures are more usual in secondary and especially primary schools, but since colleges and universities face the same threats, indefensible solutions sometimes turn up there as well. The library at the Camden campus of Rutgers, the state university of New Jersey, monitors Internet sites, because, it is claimed, a large number of patrons are youngsters who abuse their privileges (Guernsey, 1998). Thus, tuition-paying adults are hampered in their studies, placed at a distinct disadvantage, and disenfranchised, because some urban youngsters are incapable of acting responsibly. Even if monitoring or limiting were acceptable and legally warranted, this would be an untenable solution, particularly at a major research university.

Congress disagrees: In December 2000, not deterred by the blunder it had made by foisting the unconstitutional Communications Decency Act on Americans, it tried again by passing a bill "requiring virtually every school and library in the nation to install technology to protect minors from adult materials online..." (Schwartz, 2000, p. C4). This law will undoubtedly be challenged in practice and in the courts, since both source-based and key-word filtering systems are unacceptable. The former may be slightly less pernicious than the latter, but this is of no consequence. Filtering is unacceptable because it violates the First Amendment, tramples on intellectual freedom, and allows indexers' opinions, technological devices, and mechanical software products to control individual access to material that has been mounted on a global information system. These documents, images, and recordings may be inappropriate, unpleasant, politically incorrect, dangerous, seditious, repulsive, and pornographic, and we have the right to access them if we so desire. This is indeed the conclusion of the long fight carried forth in *Mainstream Loudoun v. Board of Trustees of the Loudoun County Library* (1998) in which the court ruled that the library's filtering policy was unconstitutional. But this has not deterred state legislatures and lower courts from continuing to chip away at First Amendment rights. In *Urofsky v. Gilmore*, a United States appeals court upheld a Virginia law that makes it illegal for state employees to view sexually oriented items, which in turn makes it difficult to pursue scholarly investigations; it also stifles academic freedom (Byrne, 2001). The Supreme Court refused to hear this case (Foster, 2001, January 19), despite the fact that the statute is unconstitutional.

Easy accessibility to the millions of pages and data bases on the Internet raises a related ethical problem for librarians: how to contend with plagiary. Appropriating or stealing the words or ideas of others and passing them off as one's own has always plagued educators, but the immediate availability of so much qualitatively diverse material, the ease with which complete documents can be transferred directly to a word processing program, and the fact that 70 percent of American students cheat, do not bode well for original student scholarship. Librarians are often party to this process, but their hands are tied. First, they are aware of only a small percentage of the research that occurs in their proximity; second, they are not enforcement officers or spies, and they should neither police those they help nor breach confidentiality by reporting unethical activity to anyone; and third, they have no idea how a student will reconfigure downloaded or printed material. Additionally, since institutions make hundreds of data bases available for external access, primary and secondary school as well as university students now do much of their work at home. Librarians offering telephonic or electronic help may have suspicions concerning dishonesty, but distance discipline, even if it were appropriate, would be difficult to defend, and any such action could be construed as an attempt to hamper intellectual activity. Here, as well as for the situations discussed above, it is important to keep in mind that the ongoing fight against censorship is of paramount importance because the empowered know that those who control our thoughts also control our actions.

Labeling

The American Library Association is unequivocal in its condemnation of labeling either the item or the record. Because a detailed labeling system, whether discretionary or mandatory, would complicate librarianship, confuse or unfairly influence patrons, and allow individual professionals to further their own agendas, it is considered unethical. And somehow, American librarianship and its patrons have managed to survive without labels on numerological, astrological, cosmological, extraterrestrial, quasi-scientific, homeopathic, evolutionary, sexual, or other false, misleading, or sensitive materials. Nevertheless, Mark Pendergrast (1988) bravely suggests that there are some situations in which labeling is warranted. This point of view is reaffirmed three years later by Henry Blanke, one of the authors of a pedagogical dialogue (Nesta and Blanke, 1991). Both cite publications that are factual and useful but also contain ideological propaganda as examples of material that require warnings. Looked at from a slightly different perspective, a librarian would be remiss, if, given the opportunity, he or she did not indicate to an unsuspecting or uninformed patron that the validity of *The Gourman Report* has been questioned, that Mellen's publishing methods are unusual, or that a specific encyclopedia, search engine, or website consistently garners high praise. Providing legitimate help, offering advice, or adding value cannot be construed as censorship.

An additional challenge is posed by those thinkers whose primary interest is scholarly communication; they are concerned that extremely important but distorted, contaminated, or false information is entering the data stream. Once publication in the journal or monographic literature occurs, it is often difficult or impossible to rediscover the problem and extirpate it. For this reason, *Medline* now includes corrections of errors (e.g., in prescription dosages), as well as fraudulent scholarship (e.g., conclusions based on fabricated data). Gordon Moran (1998) cites *Due Pietre Ritrovate di AMEDEO MODIGLIANI*, which appeared in 1984; this volume was sequestered after publication, but it remains in some collections despite the fact that it is a catalogue of two sculptures ascribed to Modigliani, but which in reality were created by hoaxers. Naturally, librarians cannot be responsible for the correction of errors in all disciplines, but the current stance on labeling may be counterproductive. This is a difficult topic, one that demands serious reconsideration. A detailed discussion concerning the enhancement of catalogue records can be found in Chapter 4.

During the second half of the twentieth century, society's attitude toward proscribed materials, regardless of format, has undergone dramatic changes.

Some Helpful Organizations and Periodicals

Organizations	Periodicals
American Bar Association	*Censorship News*
American Civil Liberties Union	*Civil Liberties*
American Library Association	*Freedom to Read Foundation*
Article 19: International Centre	*News*
on Censorship	*Index on Censorship*
Center for Constitutional Rights	*New Perspectives Quarterly*
Electronic Freedom Foundation	*Newsletter on Intellectual*
Feminists for Free Expression	*Freedom*
First Amendment Congress	*Our Right to Know*
Freedom to Read Foundation	*Utne Reader: The Best of the*
Fund for Free Expression	*Alternative Press*
National Coalition against	
Censorship	
Thomas Jefferson Center for the	
Protection of Free Expression	

See Harer's (1992, pp. 135ff, 227ff) *Intellectual Freedom* (from which most of the above are derived) for fuller and more balanced lists.

Case Study: A Difficult Decision

Jan Ulin, the dean of a large academic library system, had had a trying day. Three seniors, representing a small coalition of religious, feminist, minority, and concerned students, had visited her and demanded that something be done about the open access provided to all websites on the thousands of computers located in the university's libraries. They had presented an astonishingly clear, sophisticated, and reasonably argued case, even taking into account First Amendment rights and some recent countering court decisions. But they were implacable. They did not want other students, regardless of purpose, to access pornographic or hate sites.

It was difficult for Ulin to argue persuasively, because the students were already aware of the opposition's points of view. They were, after all, about to graduate after taking many indoctrinating courses in a host of disciplines. If something was not done by the next day, the students planned to go to the president, the press, and the alumni. Ulin spent the evening thinking about her options. She did not sympathize with the pornographers and hate mongers, but she was not willing to censor. She did not look forward to the morning.

Success in the fight for free and open access to theatrical, cinematic, artistic, and literary productions, iconoclastic materials, and classified government information has progressed incrementally but haphazardly as courts have ruled positively and people's attitudes have altered; these new perspectives have in turn influenced the judiciary, especially liberal Supreme Court justices such as William O. Douglas and William Brennan. The Freedom of Information Act (FOIA) opened government coffers, but information granting agencies have interpreted the law according to the dictates of the administration in power. Even when the reins are loosened, it is often impossible to get legitimately needed documents. For example, Terry Anderson, the journalist held prisoner in Lebanon for seven years, was stymied at every agency he approached for material relating directly to his case. One bureaucrat had even classified stories that Anderson had written and published!

There have been other setbacks, since special interest and religious groups have pressured lawmakers to pass repressive legislation and conservative judges sometimes issue censorious decisions. It is a sad comment indeed that at about the same time that a group of Pelham, New York, third-graders chose to write letters to a library and lead "a forum against censorship" in order to defend J. K. Rowling, author of the Harry Potter books ("third-graders," 2000), Blaise Cronin (2000), Dean of Information Science at Indiana University, informed us that common sense calls for Internet filtering and purposely insulted those librarians who disagreed.

Here is where Barbara Jones (1999) can help. In *Libraries, Access, and Intellectual Freedom,* she discusses the theoretical and legal foundations of freedom of speech and then describes precisely how one should go about writing and implementing a viable policy. Despite the current liberal ethos, we must protect ourselves and remain vigilant lest the ideologues gain the upper hand.

3

Building Collections: Books, Serials, Media

The Collection

By definition, a library, even one without walls, must collect, hold, maintain, or make accessible items of informational interest. There are collections of books or serials, films or maps, toys or textiles, CD-ROMS or online databases. These items are used on premises or circulate and electronic documents are accessed locally or globally, but there is always some tangible material involved, even if it consists primarily of digitized texts. The librarian, selector, collection developer or manager is the person responsible for the material that his or her facility makes available to its constituency. If web sites, chat rooms, bulletin boards, or electronic pen pals are the exclusive desires of users, then an intervening library is superfluous. America Online, Prodigy, or Juno can provide the communication links that will allow unlimited access to the public fora available through Internet connections. If users are befuddled or overwhelmed, they can call or email an arbitrarily chosen public or academic librarian anywhere in the United States and get some quick help. Librarians add value to whatever the novice, working alone, manages to locate.

If a physical collection is involved, then someone has to choose among the hundreds of thousands of monographs and half million serials published each year. In small libraries, one person may make all of the decisions; in a large research collection, there may be fifty or more different selectors culling out appropriate items in hundreds of academic disciplines. These specialists have subject expertise in law, medicine, linguistics, chemistry, and Mongolian studies. They hold second master's, JDs, PhDs, and countless other advanced degrees in addition to their master's in library or information science. The choices they make are based on user needs, academic programs, cost, and other identifiable criteria. Given their expertise, known requirements, and some budgetary discretion, one might at first glance think that ethical issues were not a problem. This would be a misinformed conclusion.

Communication

All media impart information, but the ethical crisis in librarianship revolves around scholarly communication. Researchers and academics communicate their ideas in many ways: through letters, at conferences, telephonically, early on over ARPANET and more recently via the Internet using email and listservs. But the primary way in which scholars reach large audiences is through the printed word. In the humanities and to a lesser extent in the social sciences, the monographic literature is extremely important, and books that are influential today may still be quite useful a decade or even a century hence. Journals do of course play a meaningful role here, but they are of utmost importance in the hard sciences, where the state of the art is extremely mercurial. As the new century unfolds, the increasing cost of books and especially periodicals and the databases that make efficient access possible is the single greatest challenge facing collection managers.

Books

Selectors choose materials in many ways. When approval plans are used, the preliminary work done in setting parameters for each disciplinary area is vitally important in the quest to control the types of documents arriving in the library. Careless or uninformed work here will have a disproportionately negative effect until it is corrected. Once the plan is set in motion, it is possible to allow volumes to insinuate themselves into the collection, even though they are unwanted, since, despite the precise parameters set up to eliminate dross or inappropriate items, these often slip through and end up on the examination shelf. If the responsible person fails to consider the hundreds of volumes that arrive each week and does not reject unwanted items, the collection will be sullied and money wasted. So, efficiency and the fulfillment of this simple responsibility is crucial. Such careful attention is less necessary when a slip plan is involved, since here only those books that are requested will arrive on site. Well-honed approval plans are efficient and beneficial, but they allow intellectual responsibility to devolve upon a mechanical system, controlled by a vendor whose primary concern is selling a product, and it does not matter whether a computer or a human being actually culls out the volume for shipping. Not all books on the culinary arts of Indonesia are appropriate for the cooking collection. Perhaps there has recently been a glut of material on this subject, maybe the book is poorly written, or it is possible that a particular collection does not require 15 items in this area. These are choices that only an on-site specialist can make.

Many selectors depend on book reviews in popular and professional publications such as *The New York Times Book Review, The New York Review of Books, Kirkus Reviews, Booklist, Library Journal, Choice,* and innumerable discipline specific journals that include critiques of new publications. These overviews indicate that an item is available and offer a concise evaluation. The same criteria that obtain for approval plan books are applied here. Since some selectors choose thousands of monographs and reference tools each year, they may be tempted to skim the comments, and this is certainly acceptable unless an extremely negative or positive evaluation is missed, and the item is incorrectly chosen or eliminated. The bibliographical data, generally offered at the head of the critique, is crucial. Some years ago, after glancing through a *Choice* review, I was about to select a volume on some chemical subject. I glanced at the price and was horrified to see that the book cost $500. The reviewer had not mentioned this. I decided that I preferred 50 volumes of poetry or fiction or biography at $10 each.

Every year, collection developers receive thousands of brochures, catalogs, and phone solicitations. These, naturally, are self-serving, since their goal is to move books from the storehouse to the library's shelves in exchange for money, but concomitantly they alert us that something exists, and they often do provide enough information so that judicious decisions can be made. A library with a very small budget should depend on reviews, but a larger collection's personnel can legitimately choose a high percentage of its holdings based on advertising. Infrequently, a human representative may call upon the selector. When making choices, the same criteria apply.

The least expensive small press volumes cost something and the most expensive reference sets are out of reach for most libraries. Publishers have the right to price their products as they see fit, but since they want to sell them, they will generally avoid alienating the purchaser. It should be kept in mind that different disciplines have very different average book prices. It would be unethical to purchase a typical children's book that cost $100, but a chemical text at this price would not be unusual. The cost should be a determining factor and when money is in short supply, it is.

When a major research university has an enormous budget, collection people may ignore cost. This is very unfair to everyone else, since a book that normally should cost very little but is exorbitantly priced may sell enough copies to appease the publisher, whereas if no one bought it, the publisher would set a more reasonable price. Consider the *Computer Science and Communications Dictionary,* a two volume compilation with a total of 2,050 pages. The cost for the set is $899. The publisher may charge an outlandish amount for these two books, but the selector is ethically obligated to at least consider alternatives. Nine hundred dollars would buy 90 ten dollar volumes. Sometimes the attempt to protect the best interests of the institution results in a debacle. When the 34 volume *Dictionary of Art* was first advertised, it cost $6,000. Since the cost was so high, since the actual publication was contingent on enough initial subscriptions to warrant production, and since the money would sit in an escrow fund or bank account for two years earning interest for Grove, I registered strong opposition to its purchase. Somehow, I prevailed and my institution did not subscribe. Some years later, when, upon publication, it was hailed as the single most important art tool to appear in the twentieth century, I changed my mind and argued for its purchase. Once again, I managed to prevail but at a great cost. We eventually paid $8,000 for this potent work. Perhaps I should have made up the difference.

Serials

Serials include reference books that come out on an ongoing basis, scholarly journals, and popular magazines. When a publisher overproduces, the selector is faced with the challenge of choosing judiciously, since except for the largest research libraries, maintaining standing orders for every set is impossible. When a publisher reproduces the same material in different guise, judicious decisions are even more important. The Gale Group purveys a host of tools useful to virtually all constituencies: primary and secondary school and undergraduate and graduate students, academics, and sophisticated researchers can all use sets such as *Contemporary Literary Criticism* or *Contemporary Authors* and profit thereby. But do we really need the same information repackaged in individual volumes or sets based on genre, theme, or ethnicity? It is convenient to have a volume limited to Hispanic authors, but because funds are limited, we lose some unique item for this convenience. Now that all of this same material is available on a data base, it is possible to search by various demarcators, but the library must be willing to pay for access. This privilege is quite expensive. It should be noted that repackaging is not limited to serials. I once selected a two volume set aimed at students published by a Gale subsidiary. When it arrived, I compared it with another work from Gale and discovered that although they were physically dissimilar, they were often textually identical. I was so annoyed that I complained. A company spokesperson meticulously explained the reasoning behind the secondary publication, did not admit culpability, but did enclose a voucher for $100. In the past, when money was more abundant, it was possible to maintain standing orders to expensive specialized serials, even though they were duplicative or unnecessary. In 1984, for example, St. Cloud State University received a new edition of the multi-volume Martindale-Hubbell directory of lawyers *every year*. It also subscribed to both the Commerce Clearing House as well as the Prentice Hall series of tax materials even though these tools do the same thing and despite the fact that we offer few tax courses and these to just a handful of students. We restructured or cancelled as much as we could.

The primary area for ethical concern is the scholarly journal. Critics, some of whom have nothing to do with librarianship, are dramatically dissatisfied with this medium, which has served us well for almost four hundred years. As early as the mid-twentieth century, this crisis in scholarly communication began to produce alternative formats including dissemination of separate articles, synopsis journals, miniprints, exclusive microform publication, and electronic offerings (Piternick, 1989). Since we now have access to an efficient electronic communication conduit, things are changing. Online journals, individual or consortial publishers, and more radical possibilities may eventually alleviate the journals crisis, although I have long held that only collection managers from various institutions working cooperatively can do anything about it in the short run. The extraordinary cost of many periodicals, especially in the hard sciences, has had four major impacts: infrequently increased serials budgets; the reallocation of monies, especially from the monograph fund; cancellation of subscriptions; and anger at what is considered price gouging and profiteering. Instead of cooperating with their primary customers, large publishers such as Elsevier, Pergamon, Springer Verlag, Kluwer, as well as smaller houses have continually increased their prices well beyond inflationary rates, purchased other publishing houses and created monopolies, dramatically multiplied the number of available periodicals, sued critics, and basically thumbed their collective noses at libraries. These publishers have acted unethically by wresting as much as they possibly could from customers who seemed to have no choice but to continue to subscribe to important publications. But by capitulating to a form of blackmail, by not convincing faculty, by not cooperating consortially, by not bringing economic pressure to bear through organizations such as ALA or ASIS, by not refusing to subscribe, librarians are equally culpable: they have wasted hundreds of millions of dollars, underwritten superfluous journals, and stimulated the greedy to continue to promulgate this horrible cycle. The cost of two thin issues of *Research in Science & Technological Education* (Taylor & Francis) is $625 and *Brain Research* (Elsevier) runs $16,344. Blackwell offers the *Journal of Political Philosophy* to individuals for $38, but libraries must pay $324, eight times as much. Differential pricing schemes ostensibly allow scholars to purchase their own subscriptions, but from the librarian's point of view, a fair price would be the lower one and institutions are penalized because they presumably have more money to share with publishers.

As the Humanities Librarian at the University of Oklahoma (1980–1984), I tried to convince colleagues at other institutions to do something, but failed dramatically. At least I was able to cancel journals based not on substantive content, which was good, but on exorbitant pricing schemes. In 1997, Purdue libraries, which "spent more than $1 million a year on Elsevier journals, cancelled 88 of its 803 subscriptions" (Orlans, 1998, p. 7). And now, librarians are uniting to solve the problem. One perhaps ineffective solution is to convince researchers to publish elsewhere or begin new but cheaper publications (Kirkpatrick, 2000). When faced with complaints publishers futilely defend their actions, promise to make alterations, or insult their clientele. A decade ago, Gillian Page (1990), director of Pageant Publishing, mustered a host of indefensible arguments in an attempt to convince librarians that we misperceive motives and bottom lines: "publishing," we are told, "is not particularly profitable..." (p. 6). There follows some mumbo jumbo concerning gross and net profit, innovations, stockholders, and so on. This is all obfuscating nonsense. If the publication of tens of thousands of scholarly journals did not generate solid profits, enormous conglomerates would stop producing them.

Page's conclusion is that "Complaints about publishers' profits are, I believe, misplaced. The real question is whether the price of a particular journal is reasonable" (p. 8). It is not, especially when it costs $12,000 or $14,000 or $16,000 per year.

The Most Expensive Journals

Brain Research	$16,344.00	Elsevier
Journal of Comparative Neurology	$14,995.00	Wiley
Nuclear Physics B	$12,113.00	Elsevier
Tetrahedron	$11,624.00	Elsevier
Tetrahedron and Tetrahedron Letters	$11,624.00	Elsevier
Journal of Applied Polymer Science	$11,570.00	Wiley
Surface Science	$9,926.00	Elsevier–Amsterdam
Journal of Chromatography A	$9,485.00	Elsevier–Amsterdam
Chemical Physics Letters	$9,029.00	Elsevier–Amsterdam
Nuclear Instruments & Meth. in Physics Res. A	$8,988.00	Elsevier
Tetrahedron Letters	$8,859.00	Elsevier Science Ltd.
Journal of Polymer Science (Part A & B)	$8,535.00	John Wiley & Sons– New York
Thin Solid Films	$8,323.00	Elsevier–Oxford
Journal of Crystal Growth	$8,111.00	Elsevier
Journal of Organometallic Chemistry	$8,103.00	Elsevier
Journal of Radioanalytical & Nuclear Chemistry	$8,041.00	Elsevier
Nuclear Physics A	$7,777.00	Elsevier
Physics Letters B	$7,595.00	Elsevier
Journal of Electroanalytical Chemistry	$7,414.00	Elsevier–Amsterdam
European Journal of Pharmacology	$7,329.00	Elsevier
Journal of Physics: Condensed Matter	$6,997.00	Institute of Physics
American Journal of Medical Genetics	$6,995.00	Wiley
Gene	$6,974.00	Elsevier–Amsterdam
Journal of Alloys and Compounds	$6,962.00	Elsevier
Nuclear Instruments & Meth. in Physics Res. B	$6,889.00	Elsevier
Hydrobiologia	$6,869.00	Kluwer
British Food Journal	$6,799.00	MCB University Press
Thermochimica Acta	$6,602.00	Elsevier
Inorganica Chimica Acta	$6,302.00	Elsevier–Lausanne

Analytica Chimica Acta	$6,210.00	Elsevier
Journal of Materials Science	$6,167.00	Kluwer
Physica C: Superconductivity	$6,010.00	Elsevier
Computer Methods in Applied Mechan. & Eng.	$5,964.00	Elsevier
Materials Science and Engineering A	$5,958.00	Elsevier
Journal of Non-Crystalline Solids	$5,928.00	Elsevier
European Physical Journal C	$5,879.00	Springer–Verlag
Neuroscience	$5,875.00	Elsevier
Journal of Molecular Structure, Theochem	$5,865.00	Elsevier–Amsterdam
International Journal of Quantum Chemistry	$5,830.00	Wiley
International Journal of Operations and Production Management	$5,729.00	MCB University Press
Journal of Magnetism and Magnetic Materials	$5,725.00	Elsevier
Biopolymers	$5,725.00	Wiley
Journal of Neuroscience Research	$5,595.00	Wiley
International Journal of Pharmaceutics	$5,589.00	Elsevier
Communications in Mathematical Physics	$5,539.00	Springer-Verlag–Berlin
Chemical Physics	$5,530.00	Elsevier–Amsterdam
Kybernetes	$5,529.00	MCB University Press
Journal of Physics A: Mathematical and General	$5,323.00	Institute of Physics
Experimental Brain Research	$5,259.00	Springer-Verlag
Carbohydrate Research	$5,253.00	Elsevier

(Database of Editors, 2000)

It bears repeating that publishers act unethically when they gouge their customers, but librarians are guilty of collusion by purchasing exorbitantly priced periodicals.

Page's analysis almost appears balanced when contrasted with the point of view articulated by Frederick A. Praeger (Winkler, 1983) in his remarks on interlibrary loan and copying practices: "All you have to do is locate one stupid librarian who is interested in buying a book, and everyone can have it" (p. 29). *Mutatis mutandis*, this would naturally apply to periodicals as well.

Access to the periodical literature, even in smaller public libraries, is now gained not through traditional hard copy indexes, which were sold via pricing schemes that made them affordable to most collections, but rather through electronic databases, in the recent past on CD-ROM and now on the Internet. The advantages of Internet access are so multitudinous that the negative aspects are glossed over or ignored. We have little patience with those who lament the loss of traditional scholarly methodologies, fragmented knowledge, settling for whatever appears on the computer screen, full-text that eliminates letters, editorials, advertisements, and graphics, lack of integrity, errors, slow response time, crashes, and other computer mediated problems. But if convenience really does outweigh its counterparts, pricing remains a real ethical concern. These databases are distressingly expensive. Five or 10 thousand dollars per year is typical and 15 or 20 thousand dollars is not unusual. Lexis-Nexis continually increases its price so that my institution now pays $46,000 per year for this service (and this is one of the very few databases for which the publisher does not allow broad external access). All of ISI's database packages are out of the realm of possibility for most libraries; the *Web of Science,* for example, would cost St. Cloud State University with its 15,000 students more than $100,000 per year, and this does not include some major initial costs. When these databases offer full-text, when the articles can be printed inexpensively at school or for nothing at home, when they can be downloaded and manipulated (thus making plagiary so much more convenient), it is impossible to argue against subscriptions, despite the cost. The state of Minnesota pays the Gale Group almost two million dollars per year for access to all of the full-text data bases contained on *InfoTrac.* If faculty, teachers, students, and public library patrons lose this service in leaner times, it will be a real disaster. Acclimatization to online indexes, especially those that contain the complete text of the located documents, results in a psychological and physical unwillingness to track down materials that exist only in hard copy, in bound volumes, and especially in microformat. These additional tasks are incomprehensibly onerous to a generation bred on the convenience of instant gratification. But those who favor electronic access over all other necessities harm the integrity of a collection, which also includes hard copy reference tools, monographs, films, maps, recordings, software and many other formats, both for current users and for those who will come along in 20 or 40 or 60 years. If online data bases were reasonably priced, they would be just one other item to be considered, but because they cost so much, one may have to sacrifice a decade's worth of commercial and documentary videos for a single subscription to *Psycinfo,* which is used by only a small percentage of most libraries' patrons.

Media

The third major area in which libraries collect is media, including videos, CDs, tapes, slides, and software. Each of these formats requires a different piece of equipment to make the material accessible. These devices are expensive and must be maintained. When a new format arrives, e.g., video disk, a piece of appropriate equipment must be purchased. When formats such as celluloid film or vinyl recordings become outmoded, the player is no longer produced and eventually it becomes impossible to view the film or listen to the record. These and other types of preservation problems are discussed in chapter 8; here it is sufficient to note that it is unethical to commit a large percentage of one's budget to a format that will no longer be usable just a few years later. Expressed in a more positive way, one might merely insist that libraries hire technicians capable of maintaining outmoded equipment even though replacement parts are no longer available.

Media present some problems that books and journals do not. The fair use clause of the current copyright law allows for the reproduction of printed materials for educational usage. But this exclusion does not apply when patrons are interested in retaining a complete copy of a film or CD, since personal reproduction makes it unnecessary to purchase the item, thus causing financial loss to the publisher or artist. Once patrons have borrowed the item, it is impossible for the library's personnel to obviate the possibility of copying a video or burning a CD. Nor should this be our responsibility. Additionally, the evolution of Internet storage and retrieval modalities, such as Napster, have affirmed the public's lackadaisical attitude toward authors' rights. It is just too convenient to consider kidnapping through Napster anything but acceptable practice despite the obvious fact that it is outright theft. Although a major international conglomerate has aligned itself with Napster's owner, the problem remains, since similarly empowered websites will continue to flourish, making copyright infringement a simple task. One only has to recall that despite the fearsome, threatening FBI notice that appears at the head of commercial videos, viewers copy them with impunity.

Concluding Remarks

In addition to all of the considerations discussed above, selectors must defend the collection against those who would pressure us to purchase or collect materials that are, for one reason or another, inappropriate. Vendors, sales representatives, and their accompanying brochures,

---

Case Study: The Money Is All Gone

After five years of increasing budgets, Larry Inope, the director of the Ron Valley College library, had just learned that drastic cuts were mandatory for the next fiscal year. Despite its small size, Ron Valley has a superb biology program, and the percentage of its graduates admitted to medical school is one of the highest in the nation. Because money had been so replete, the periodicals selection committee had instituted subscriptions to some very expensive biology and chemistry journals and databases including *Biosis* and ISI's *Web of Science*. Now that funds had to be drastically cut, Inope was faced with an insoluble dilemma: Should he eliminate the monograph budget, cancel subscriptions to hundreds of inexpensive humanities and social science periodicals, deprive professors and students of the new materials they had been so grateful to have, or cut a faculty line by firing an untenured librarian? No matter what he and the faculty decided, it would generate bad feelings, and the intellectual life of the campus would suffer. He decided to approach the president directly, but feared that this would be a futile gesture.

---

catalogues, and advertisements come immediately to mind, but since they operate at our behest, it is not too difficult to just say no. As I observe in *Ethical Challenges in Librarianship* (Hauptman, 1988), when faculty members or researchers in special libraries attempt to unduly and unfairly influence acquisitions, it is up to the selector to mediate an acceptable middle ground. Just because an individual professor specializes in biochemical computing does not mean that the library must acquire every item he or she requests.

It is unusual to place collection development within an ethical context, but in an incisive and courageous essay, Kenneth Frazier (1999) argues that many of the choices that selectors make have strong ethical implications, especially in the current repressive environment that is characterized by extremely expensive materials, intellectual restriction, and enormous global publishers. Frazier discusses three cases (the Gordon & Breach lawsuits, the *History of European Ideas* debacle, and interlibrary loan suppression), and advocates a newly restructured, disintermediated scholarly communication system, which I allude to above. A step in this direction is the founding of the Scholarly Publishing and Academic Resources Coalition (SPARC) (Werner, 2000), which has almost 200 members; it is attempting to encourage publishers to produce alternative and less expensive materials, and the American Chemical Society is a participant. This is an excellent idea and perhaps my pessimism is unwarranted, but I also think that this may simply compound the problem by cloning more and more journals that many research libraries will simply add to their collections without canceling the expensive commercial progenitors.

Jane Schweinsburg (1995) insists that "Completely unbiased selection is not humanly possible…" (p. 37). Nevertheless, ethical selection policies require that we choose appropriate materials for the collection and its patrons, while scrupulously attempting to ignore social and personal prejudices that may seduce us into censoring unacceptable, taboo, sexually oriented, dangerous, expensive, and even reprehensible items. Concomitantly, we must choose judiciously so that in our attempt to be fair we do not build only the Holocaust denial, pornography, or multicultural collections at the expense of more traditional fare. And of course we must consider cost. Canceling one $46,000 database would allow us to purchase or subscribe to hundreds of monographs and periodicals. Balanced selection is the key to well-rounded collections for current users and future generations.

4

• • • • • • • • • • • • •

Technical Services:
Acquisitions and Cataloging

The work done in technical service areas including checking, order-ing, recording, unpacking, stamping, copy cataloging, classifying, label-ing, and the like is often, though not always, performed by paraprofessionals or students. In a smaller facility, one librarian will do all of these things, whereas in a large research institution, these tasks may be divided among hundreds of employees. As in the case of selection, at first superficial glance, it hardly seems possible that ethical considerations would play more than a minimal role here. But, lamentably, wherever human beings are found, unethical activity can manifest itself.

Acquisitions

An employee has a major responsibility to protect the best interests of the institution. Carelessness that results in extreme waste constitutes an ethical breach. Individuals are entitled to make an occasional error, but ongoing mistakes that result in thousands of dollars in lost monies are unacceptable, and necessitate a change in procedure or disciplinary action. During the early 1980s, an employee at the University of Oklahoma missed the entry or misread the catalog and reordered two items that were already part of the collection. If these had been $30 monographs, it would have been of little consequence, but they were Lasso and Lully scores and cost the library thousands of dollars, money that was sorely needed for other materials. Meticulousness and efficiency are far more important than we care to admit, until we find ourselves on an operating table.

Protection of new books and serials is a paramount concern. It is mooted that three quarters of all theft in libraries is perpetrated by employees. Even if this is a hyperbolic assessment, unstripped items should be fully protected, especially from the public. In some facilities, it is impossible for patrons to find their way into the acquisitions area, but in smaller libraries or in geographical locations where crime is uncommon, anyone can wander in. The facilitation of theft is not only unethical, it is also illegal and subject to prosecution. The protection of new materials is an important responsibility of the librarians or the director of the division. It may seem unfair or foolish to the unconcerned, but unstripped, uncataloged material should never leave the area, even though someone has been anxiously waiting to read the volume for six months. Library employees or faculty should not have special privileges.

Vendors vie for our business in many ways. The conflicts of interest that arise when acquisitions personnel accept shopping bags full of lagniappes at conferences can be eliminated by ignoring what amounts to insignificant trinkets. More conflicting are the breakfasts and especially serious dinners that are sometimes provided. The easy solution here is to refuse to participate or to pay for what one eats, even from one's own pocket. Saving 15 or 20 dollars hardly compensates for suspicions or accusations. If the acquisitions librarian enjoys an 1845 Rothchild with dinner, he should indulge on his own resources. The moment one accepts a gift, the moment one enhances a relationship with someone who desires one's business, humans are no longer capable of making objective decisions, and choosing a vendor may ultimately be based on criteria that are not necessarily beneficial to the institution. This might appear to be an insignificant and easily soluble problem, but abuses are probably more widespread than we care to admit. More than a decade ago, Christian Boissonnas (1987) devoted seven long pages to a fictional scenario in which conflict of interest is illuminated. More recently, Peter Schanck (1999) reaffirmed the admonition that we must take care to avoid even the appearance of a conflict. I am fairly certain that although government officials are now severely proscribed from accepting gratuities or bribes, librarians continue to accept sometimes valuable gifts.

Acquisitions librarians should not accept periodicals from patrons if the purpose is to circumvent the dual pricing system discussed above. Despite what amounts to publisher dishonesty, allowing patrons to present their journals to the collection is highly unethical, especially since subscribers often sign a pledge that they will not do this. Acquisitions personnel should never claim materials that have arrived but are later lost or stolen. The correct procedure here would be to purchase a replacement copy, at a reasonable price, one would hope. We should insist that vendors or individual publishers include a listing of materials and their prices in the same package that contains the order. This can serve as a checklist that the books or videos actually arrived; then the listing can be used to verify payment. Cryptic invoices forwarded prior or subsequent to shipment should be returned without payment, otherwise there is a good chance that mistakes or purposeful deception on the part of publishers or vendors will result in unnecessary or redundant payments. Standing order and periodical payments may be handled differently, but the invoices should be unequivocally clear so that we understand the billing.

Acquisitions or some other division has always negotiated lease agreements with companies that do not sell their products. Some directories are leased, as is the Rand McNally *Commercial Atlas*. Wiseman's films are leased for five years at which time the agreement is renewed or the film, *Titicut Follies*, for example, is returned. Because these agreements have dealt with books or films, the usage or duplication of which is easy to understand, few complications occur, and generally speaking a contract that is fair to both parties is easily drawn. There is probably no negotiation here, since the owner simply lays out the requirements and the librarian either accepts or rejects them. As materials have become available in various electronic formats, lease agreements have become more prevalent. Full text data bases offer a plethora of new possibilities to users, and producers have attempted to cover every contingency in their agreements, thus reaping as much profit as possible while concomitantly stifling access whenever it appears to circumvent some form of remuneration. These leases are now extremely complicated and are written to the sole advantage of the producer. Once the agreement is signed, once the product is accessible, once the libraries' constituency acclimates itself to its usage,

---

Cryptic Invoices

This is an invoice requesting $432:

MFP-MARCH 1989 REV W/TOP COVER VOL IAPT2 R#81 & MARCH 89 CUM SP & REV/V8-8C R#44

(Kingsley & Berwick, 1990, p. 27)

once patrons can no longer function without it, the producer can raise the price dramatically. Here we are not talking about inflationary indices nor the overweening desire to increase profits by a percentage point or two. A $7,000 web-based data base can go to $15,000 within a year; $20,000 products can jump to $46,000. The only solution to these dramatic price increases is to sign long term contracts, which we are naturally loath to do.

Much more onerous are the abrogations of fair usage that these data base producers demand. Interlibrary loan offices in public and academic libraries may copy material from printed books and periodicals as long as their procedures conform to the current copyright law. Fair use allows for broad dissemination of purchased materials. Patrons may copy printed items as well as texts that appear on computer screens both at the library or in their homes. They may also email electronic documents to other locations. But many data base producers disallow copying by interlibrary loan offices for dissemination to those who do not have access to the data base. We should never have agreed to this subtle distinction, for it drastically limits information dissemination and sets a theoretical precedent that could be retrospectively applied to hard copy materials. It may come to pass that instructors or students will be threatened with long prison terms should they copy a few pages from *Time* or *Cell.* This type of educational copying is almost always done for convenience: it is just easier and more efficient to have a copy that can be read and reread at home rather than forcing one's way through everything in the library, jotting down inaccurate notes, and leaving out the most important parts. Such copying is not meant to save money on subscriptions nor does it deprive the publisher or the author of revenue. The same is true of electronic texts. Just because someone requires a brief article does not mean that his home library will be willing or able to lease an inappropriate $20,000 data base. (See Chapter 10 for more on copyright.)

Cataloging

Before the advent of the CIP program, The *National Union Catalog* (NUC) served librarians who acquired new material, but who did not want to do their own cataloging and classification. Naturally, in order for this to work, the item already had to be in the *NUC* and the cataloger had to have access to the many hundreds of large volumes. Then along came OCLC and other national utilities, and once institutions outside of Ohio were able to join, catalogers could easily pick up the data they required by calling the item up on their computer screens.

In the early days, this could have been considered an unethical practice, since those who entered the record did the work and those who picked it up were taking something and not compensating the creator. But the ethos has changed and the utilities now consist of theoretically equal members who give and take cooperatively. Furthermore, CIP data allow paraprofessionals to create serviceable card catalog or OPAC entries with very little effort. But ethical problems continue to arise precisely because it is so easy. Only a careful scrutiny of the book or film or slide set will confirm that both the description as well as the call number are correct. In a financially strapped environment, no supervisor will allow employees to spend time confirming the accuracy of previously created records, especially when they come from the Library of Congress. If an error is found, the worker will make a correction in the local record, but may fail to alter the utility's entry. The thousands of online catalogs that may have incorporated the mistake will continue to purvey false data to users. Other librarians or patrons who find errors may hesitate to bring them to someone's attention because it interrupts what they are doing or because they do not want to annoy or offend. But if no one alerts the appropriate authority, the error continues to confuse or obfuscate, despite the fact that it has been detected.

It may appear to matter very little that a book or video is misclassified, since a search of the OPAC will yield the false call number, which

---

Errors

Library of Congress Cataloging-in-Publication Data

Michalson, Gordon E., 1948–
    Kant and the problem of God / Gordon E. Michalson, Jr.
        p. cm.
    Includes bibliographical references and index.
    ISBN 0-631-21219-1 (alk. paper).—ISBN 0-631-21220-5
(pbk. : alk. paper)
        1. Kant, Immanuel, 1724–1804—Religion. 2. Religion—Philosophy.
I. Title.
ZA3225.C48   1998
210'.92—dc21   98-33148
                                                                    CIP

This is a reproduction of the CIP included in the Michalson volume. The call number is incorrect. Instead of locating the book with others dealing with religious philosophy, it is placed in the new ZA class along with materials on information, the Internet, and related matters.

nevertheless will lead to the item (unless it is misshelved). But researchers often locate one or two pertinent call numbers for a topic and then go directly to the shelves to glance at a number of volumes. When a given item with an incorrect call number is shelved hundreds of stacks away, it is inaccessible to a patron engaged in serendipitous searching. (It is worth observing that this type of discovery is of course impossible in closed stacks, which most frequently exist in research collections: undergraduates, for example, are sometimes not allowed to enter areas where graduate students and faculty are welcome. The main research branch of the New York Public Library, the Library of Congress, the Bodleian at Oxford, and special and archival collections all proscribe entry into the stacks, an understandable policy that nevertheless limits access, since patrons will not be able to scan all of the material nor will most researchers be willing to call for hundreds of potentially useful items.)

Language is destiny. The use of misleading, obfuscating, or offensive terminology is indeed deplorable, and the primary ethical challenge in cataloging is the extirpation of these unacceptable subject headings. But it is equally important to observe that the substitution of politically correct nomenclature is just as harmful; referring to those who are healthy as non-disabled only harms the cause. Euphemisms change descriptors, not attitudes or abilities, and sometimes those who suffer are more offended by good linguistic intentions than by blatant terminology. Nevertheless, during the last third of the twentieth century, Sanford Berman mounted a one man campaign both at the Hennepin County Library as well as at the Library of Congress to change or expand official headings. Although LC catalogers only begrudgingly cooperated, alterations have been made, and many materials are now more accessible or less offensive because of his efforts. Not surprisingly though, some things remain the same. In *Prejudices and Antipathies,* Berman (1971) carefully lays out a host of terms that deserve alteration or extirpation. It should be noted that although he is entitled to a personal opinion on any given word or phrase, he backs his point of view up with impeccable scholarly references. Herewith follow some examples. The Rogues and vagabonds cross-reference from GIPSIES is gone from the 1999 edition of the *Library of Congress Subject Headings,* but GYPSIES is still there, despite the fact that these people prefer Roma or Sinti. MAMMIES was pejorative in 1971, but it can still be found in the 1999 edition. JEWISH CRIMINALS remains, but LC did alter BANKS AND BANKING—JEWS to JEWISH BANKERS. Is this supposed to be an improvement, when there are no subdivisions for Daoists, Hindus, or any other religious or ethnic group? SOCIETY, PRIMITIVE is gone, but PRIMITIVE SOCIETIES replaced it.

Berman's well-argued position was apparently ignored. Naturally, derogatory expressions for Italians, Hispanics, Jews, African Americans, and other groups are expunged, but KAFFIR still turns up in 1999. The "see also" reference to terrorism is gone from ANARCHISM AND ANARCHISTS, but inexplicably JEWISH ANARCHISTS has been added. FREE LOVE continues to refer to concubinage and DISCIPLINE OF CHILDREN still appears where one might expect to find it. The LC cataloging supervisors make changes as they see fit. (See Hope Olson's (2001) essay for additional discussion.)

In a 1983 essay included in *Worth Noting*, Berman (1988) lists LC terminology for things that are commonly referred to quite differently. This has always been a challenge for people using a manual card catalog. Now that key word searching is possible on OPACs, the situation is less critical, but if the patron's input does not match the recorded subject or key words, than the search will yield nothing despite the fact that there is appropriate material in the collection. A few of Berman's examples should suffice to show how misleading catalog headings can be.

LC	*Common*
CLOTHING, COLD WEATHER	WINTER CLOTHING
DWELLINGS	HOUSES
MICROMYS MINUTUS	HARVEST MOUSE

Berman also includes many older as well as more recent terms that were not available in 1983 in the LC listing. Since the legitimizing of subject headings is under the control of a conservative organization, there will always be problems similar to those described above. Nevertheless, it is ethically malfeasant to refuse to correct unacceptable terminology or include useful headings that would help to make material more accessible. The examples throughout this discussion have come from the Library of Congress compilation, but the *Sears List of Subject Headings* also has had many of the same problems.

A catalog entry for a commercial or documentary film, now generally produced on video cassette or disk except for theater showings, where celluloid film is still used, includes a brief descriptive note that summarizes the production. This usually appears on an OPAC, but it would also be available in a traditional card catalog. Outside of specialized or archival collections, similar descriptive notes are never offered for book entries, despite the confusion that may occur in broad categories such as historical and fictional accounts. Notes that describe, clarify, explain, adduce, or apprise would be useful generally and invaluable when the item is problematic. But as discussed above, this would fall under the rubric of labeling, whether the note was included in the catalog entry, in the item, or in

---

Case Study: Political Correctness Is Not the Issue

Hillary ten Low has worked at the Library of Congress for 12 years. Her cataloging is beyond reproach, but alerted and sensitized to demeaning, confusing, and useless LC subject headings that are altered or eliminated only under duress, she has begun making some small changes. She indicated this to two colleagues and her supervisor. Her colleagues agreed that some terms do require emendation, but were not courageous enough to stand up for ten Low; they certainly did not make any changes of their own.

Her supervisor, who happened to belong to a much abused ethnic minority, sympathized with ten Low's crusade, but indicated that her tactics were unacceptable, and that the entries would have to be corrected. Ten Low refused. Over a period of three weeks, the situation worked its way up the hierarchy to the head of cataloging and eventually to the Librarian of Congress. It was a major brouhaha, since most of the officials agreed that the terminology was problematic, but could not bring themselves to alter professional mandates. The administration called for a meeting. They hoped to keep all of this away from the media.

---

both locations. Few critics have advocated a change here. In 2000, Leonard Hitchcock published a ground-breaking article in which he offers some hypothetical notes along with a strong defense for the inclusion of such information in book entries. His choices are apposite and act as exemplars for categories where comments would be a true service to both laypersons and scholars. He includes Wilkomirski's *Fragments,* a Holocaust account that turned out to be fictitious; an abridged edition of Swift's *Gulliver's Travels,* which also happens to be bowdlerized; Velikovsky's *Worlds in Collision,* the cause of a mid-twentieth century cultural brouhaha that has not yet fully subsided; Richard's *Principles of Literary Criticism,* an influential study; and *The Crisis in Drug Prevention,* whose editor, David Boaz, was an officer of the Cato Institute, an ideologically driven think-tank. Hitchcock then presents four pages of reasoned commentary on the occasional necessity for such scope notes. He indicates that they would be technically possible, contributed by some staff members, controlled by an editor, not always required, and a breach of the "Library Bill of Rights," which, he claims, occurs frequently. The goal here is to inform, not to restrict, and as such it is laudable.

These informational enhancements would be beneficial especially to the uninitiated, and despite Hitchcock's bold admission, they could be included without abrogating the principles of free expression and balanced access that the anti-labeling statement attempts to protect. There will, naturally, be both inadvertent and purposeful abuses of catalog notes but that is hardly a valid reason for stifling their use. It is incumbent upon librarians to offer value-added services; this is an extremely helpful possibility.

Cataloging is a demanding, repetitious, and sometimes tedious task. In order to do an excellent job, one that produces a correctly cataloged and classified item in virtually every case, a person must scrupulously study and learn the many rules and conventions. This is impossible to do on one's own and so as Sheila Intner (1993) points out, it is necessary to at least take some classes in an appropriate program. She implies or indicates that it is unethical to do minimal cataloging, to let large quantities of material remain uncataloged for long periods, to allow untutored copy catalogers to create original entries, to create inaccurate records, and to discriminate against non-print materials. I agree. Acquisitions and cataloging are the structural backbone upon which a patron relies in order to efficiently locate what he or she needs. There is no room here for ethical lapses.

5

. . . .

Access Services

Access is encouraged or proscribed in accordance with the theoretical foundations that undergird librarianship, and the practical applications that individual information professionals implement. The object of any collection is to make materials available to the user and that is what librarians generally attempt to do. Even the extraordinary artifacts now on display at the Morgan Library in New York were originally created to be read, and collected to be savored. Morgan must have occasionally taken down a Gutenberg Bible or the serial sections of a Dickens novel and glanced at the pages, fondled the bindings, or touched the gold leaf. Just thirty years ago, legitimate scholars could visit British collections and call for the *Lindisfarne Gospels* or the *Beowulf* manuscript and study the original documents. Although that policy has changed and superb facsimiles are now tendered, access to material is still the goal of even the most esoteric collection. An unread or unviewed artifact may as well not exist.

Access services is similar to circulation; it provides users with checkout and reserve materials, and may also protect video and audio tapes, compact disks, other non-print items, as well as equipment such as television monitors, projectors, computers, and so on. Students, in an academic setting, and paraprofessionals, in a public library, often perform the various tasks that help access services to function efficiently. This is one of the few areas in a library where money may change hands or where desperate students may attempt to manipulate the system because they wish to read something that has been placed on two-hour reserve or because they owe an inordinate sum, since they failed to return a reserved book or article promptly. Workers have access to patron names, addresses, social security and other identifying numbers, and sensitive circulation data. There are many possibilities here for ethical transgressions.

All faculty, staff, paraprofessional, student, and part-time help should be fully apprised of the procedures and precautions necessary to protect sensitive information. Once data are no longer needed, they should be expunged. Maintaining patron records beyond their usefulness is unethical because upon issuance of a subpoena, the files may end up in court and in the media; such breaches of patron confidentiality should be assiduously avoided. Unnecessary access to patron files must be strongly discouraged in the same way that the IRS, which in the past tacitly tolerated intrusions, now discourages curious employees from scanning files—by firing them. No employee should ever reveal who has checked out an item, even though such information may be innocently requested in order to facilitate some important task. Library staff may contact a patron when

---

How to Protect Confidentiality

Libraries sometimes operate under the auspices of organizations that by their very nature misuse or abuse data and information or violate confidentiality. We do not have to approbate, sanction, nor condone such activity.

1. Do not use social security numbers as identifiers.
2. Expunge circulation records as soon as possible.
3. Do not reveal proscribed data or information to relatives, instructors, directors, deans, provosts, presidents, trustees, board members, police, FBI or CIA agents, or anyone else who arrives without a warrant signed by a judge. Even then, one should refer the inquiry to a supervisor who may, at his or her discretion, refuse to comply.
4. Protect the identity of interlibrary lenders.
5. Do not comment on patron matters for pleasure.
6. When it is necessary to discuss confidential material, e.g., a difficult reference query, mask the patron's identity.
7. Do not store sensitive data on open electronic systems, in unlocked file cabinets, on desk tops, or in publicly accessible baskets.
8. Protect patron data as you would want a medical records manager or banker to protect information that pertains to your health or finances.

an emergency need arises. For example, if a professor desperately requires a video to show to her class later in the afternoon, a supervisor can certainly try to retrieve it. It is possible that the person who legitimately has the item may refuse to return it, but at least someone made an effort. Librarianship is, after all, a pure manifestation of the service economy; refusing to help would be a dereliction of one's duty.

Because stressful situations often arise, especially in a large, busy academic setting, employees may have to deal with anxious, annoyed, angry, or even dangerous patrons. It is best to attempt to placate those who are upset, even though they may be wrong. First, no one wants to be involved in an altercation, fight, or civil suit; second, sometimes the person has a legitimate complaint and it is better to resolve it immediately than to allow it to work its way up to the director, the board, the president, or the media. It takes many good deeds to make up for one case of bad publicity. The president or the public tends to recall a single negative instance and easily forgets the thousands of positive interactions. Third, our goal is to serve, and a dissatisfied patron is a service failure.

Most academic libraries are open until midnight; some stay open 24 hours a day. After the administrators, faculty members, staff, and most student help retire for the night, it is necessary to maintain a skeleton staff generally consisting of students. It is mandatory to have either a responsible, well-trained adult or a security officer on hand at all times. In case of emergency, one or two young students may panic and unnecessary harm can occur. Potential emergencies include fire, flood, tornado, earthquake, electrical outages, electronic crashes, altercations, heart attacks, severe sickness, and lunacy.

At first glance, it may appear that anyone can call 911, the campus or local police, the fire department, or maintenance, but if a student worker is threatened, he or she may just leave the building. And shelvers may not understand the subtleties of cardio-pulmonary resuscitation. If an academic campus and its facilities do not take security seriously, adequately provide for emergencies, and truly protect their constituency, they ultimately will pay a very high price. Libraries require extra protection because they often house hundreds or even thousands of strangers who may be anxious or inebriated; they contain valuable, sometimes priceless materials; and except for some private and urban institutions, anyone can wander in including the homeless, the dishonest, and the psychotic. For the heads of libraries to fail to allocate funds for real security, even in a comparatively safe environment, is a dereliction of duty. This applies to public libraries as well, although they may have a number of professionals on duty until they close, usually no later than nine or ten at night.

Those who work in access services are often faced with small problems that cause patrons big frustrations. In an automated library, it is necessary to have an identification card that allows for electronic scanning. Patrons, especially adolescents in a public library and young students at college, may not carry cards or even money with them. When personnel interpret the rules stringently, they will refuse to allow these people to check out long-term materials or even two-hour reserve items. Biometric identification is already in use in many sensitive environments and there undoubtedly will come a time, despite the best efforts of Libertarians, when patrons will stand proxy for their cards: they will be scanned, probed, read, or photographed. But until such measures are implemented in libraries, it behooves personnel to act in a humane and flexible way. I am not advocating the general abrogation of necessary rules but rather case by case consideration. If a cardless student promises to read an article nearby and return it in an hour, it may be possible to accommodate her. Naturally, there will be times when it is impossible to help, but the service ethic under which we operate insists that we always attempt to fulfill needs, delimit frustration, and connect patrons with the items of their choice whether these are books, journals, tapes, software, electronic equipment, or meeting rooms.

Access Proscriptions

Censorship and inappropriate selection limit access. So do fees. Theoretically, we should never charge, but in actuality, there are very few services that are truly free. In the public library environment, municipal or state taxes pay for purchases, salaries, and overhead. In academic institutions, taxes, tuition, activity fees, and endowments that derive from gifts pay for library services including what students think of as "free" printing or copying. Reproduction, rentals, in-depth analyses, and overdues should all be free, otherwise some patrons will hesitate to avail themselves of a given service. Naturally, they are not, and in an academic facility that charges for computer and microformat printing, copying, and overdue items, a student could theoretically spend each day's lunch money to cover various services. Public libraries should not charge fees because some of the clientele cannot afford to pay for food or rent; they will assuredly be delimited in their informational needs, if they are charged for services. And since students at academic institutions have already paid tuition, they should not be coerced into supporting the generation of profits. At a cost of three cents per page, it is possible, for example, to provide leased copy machines for patron use. Instead, libraries charge eight or ten or even fifteen cents per copy. These charges generate a profit that is used to purchase new equipment or software. Theoretically, we advocate free service; in reality we often levy sometimes exorbitant fees.

The public and, to a lesser extent, the academic library are places where the frequently discussed digital divide can be bridged. Despite the denials of middle-class sociologists, there really are people who cannot afford the luxury of a computer, printer, or phone connection; nor do some of these folks have the need or motivation to acquire the equipment and learn how to use, maintain, and repair it when it crashes. A surprising number of people and even students still do not use, let alone own, the requisite technologies to send email messages, access the Internet, do esoteric computations, or plot trajectories on geographic information systems. Libraries provide the equipment as well as ongoing instruction in the use of basic as well as sophisticated searching techniques and software applications. Anyone who has the desire to learn and then to apply his or her knowledge to access information or create textual documents or multimedia programs can do so, often with no direct cost.

Before the Internet ostensibly made all information accessible, interlibrary loan (ILL) provided patrons with books and free photocopies of unavailable articles, all within a matter of days. In reality, ILL continues to provide invaluable service to anyone who requires something that the home library does not own. ILL must adhere to copyright law, but otherwise it is free to provide unlimited materials to patrons. In an educational setting, the fair use doctrine protects traditional requests. The current status of electronic materials and their duplication may not be settled until judicial decisions set some precedents, since librarians believe that they have the right to reproduce electronic documents and publishers insist that they may not. Budgetary, age, and status proscriptions that are sometimes placed on patrons are ethically unacceptable. At the same time, users should be apprised that each transaction costs a substantial sum in processing fees. Some balance should be sought between an unblinking fulfillment of hundreds of superfluous requests and an officious reluctance to provide required items.

Public and academic libraries have an intrinsic commitment to all patrons. Some people have special problems, but this does not alter nor obviate the commitment. Since individuals, bureaucrats, and institutions often lack compassion or are incapable of providing adequate service without some stimulus, Congress passed the Americans with Disabilities Act, which, among other things, mandates that provision be made for persons who cannot operate in a normal environment. Libraries have complied with both the letter and the spirit of the law, but sometimes major

---

Case Study: Computer Frustration

The large, urban public library that Amiel visits fulfills all ADA mandated requirements. People confined to wheelchairs have excellent
ingress through mechanically operated doors; the elevators are new and
easy to operate; the aisles are wide and accommodating; and there are
three specially equipped computer stations, all of which give access to
the OPAC, more than 20 data bases, software programs, and the unfiltered Internet. But Amiel is frequently frustrated because the stations he
is able to use are almost never available. Naturally, other disabled people use them, but sometimes, despite the warning signs, people without
special needs are frantically typing and Amiel, who is shy, is loath to create a disturbance. Twice during the last month, one station was empty
as he rolled into view, but then he discovered that the computer had
crashed. And to make matters as bad as possible, when he does manage
to get a station, it is physically onerous to type. He had requested that
the library purchase voice activated software and install the computer in
a separate room so that his articulations would not bother other patrons.
They were looking into this possibility, slowly.

---

challenges and frustrations remain. Compassion and special regard would
solve many of the problems that occur. A blind student, for example, cannot locate a book or journal in the stacks. An easy solution is to retrieve
what is needed and photocopy the required pages. Not every student
worker or staff and faculty member is empowered or willing to do this.
Superior service requires resensitization and the alteration of rules. The
disabled are stymied, frustrated, or harmed by physical impediments,
inadequate equipment, and bad attitudes. People who are in total command of their bodies and environments do not realize how difficult it is
to perform the basic tasks that allow one to function normally: tying
shoelaces, paying for purchases, seeing obstacles, using a restroom, or
accessing a computer may present insurmountable obstacles to the disabled. Some of the tasks that one must perform in the course of researching a topic or fulfilling an assignment are difficult and frustrating for any
young student; the problems are magnified for someone who is unable to
see or hear or walk or speak clearly.

Naturally, we must provide wheelchair accessible stations, enlarging
and voice activated computers, scanning equipment that allows for
machine articulation of texts and Internet sites, and any other hardware
and software that help those patrons who cannot avail themselves of unen-
hanced equipment. At least one employee should specialize in this area;
he or she should be well-versed in the use of the equipment, be willing
and able to train colleagues and users, and be especially sensitized to the

special problems that can occur. Ironically, the many new technologies available for searching, online course work, word processing, and computing sometimes create barriers for the disabled, whereas these extraordinary technologies should act as enhancements and ease the plight of those who cannot function in a normal environment. Alternative modes of access should be employed; for example, if a course's required web site offers audio instruction, this should be translatable into a visually accessible mode for those who are hearing impaired. The creation and implementation of local and global web sites is, naturally, beyond the control of library personnel, but, as Veronica Rouse (1999) observes, it is possible for a librarian to work with instructors in order to incorporate appropriate technologies that will make the online material easily accessible to the disabled. Rouse discusses equipment and design guidelines and offers some useful ideas. Obviously, public and academic library web pages should be designed with all users in mind. And as highly specialized hardware or software becomes available, it should be purchased, not merely because the law so stipulates, but rather because this allows us to fulfill our commitment to complete access for everyone, not just those who happen to be mobile or sighted or able to manipulate keyboards or other tactile devices without any problems. Additionally, in our quest to accommodate the physically impaired we may relegate the learning disabled to second class status; sometimes, students with dyslexia, mild aphasia, or attention disorders require special technologies, extra assistance, or special consideration. Instead, both the learning and physically disabled may be put off, shunted around, and provided primarily with excuses for non-existent or inoperative equipment. Finally, since some minorities are underrepresented in the profession (McCook, 2000), there may be a deleterious effect on service to diverse populations. On the other hand, a balanced appraisal must include the fact that American libraries *have* served diverse populations with care and understanding. For example, in 1950, in order to reach the English language books on the second floor of the Chatham Square branch of the New York Public Library, I first had to pass through the Chinese language collection. Naturally! This branch served Chinatown's population.

Access is a simple word with extremely diverse implications. In order to fully, fairly, and ethically provide for all users in all environments, we must recommit ourselves to the principles upon which librarianship is founded. Then we must act as if each patron is the only one who counts.

6

. . . .

Reference

Reference is the area in which the most frequent professional-patron interactions in librarianship occur, and this is equally true in public, academic, special, or archival collections. It is here that one must bring to bear incisive communication skills, psychological insight, a keen and curious mind, extraordinary substantive knowledge, electronic searching abilities and techniques, and a well developed ethical sensitivity. This at least is the general if hyperbolic picture offered in the literature. In reality, much reference work can be performed by bright and motivated undergraduates, paraprofessionals, or graduate students working on master's degrees in librarianship. And that is why many institutions now offer tiered service, which allows the simpler queries to be culled out; only the more difficult, substantive questions are referred to an expert either in information provision or in a specific discipline.

This assessment should not cause any undue anguish; similar conclusions can be drawn in most other professions. It takes ten years to become a licensed physician, but an adolescent can ride an ambulance and help to save lives; he or she can learn all that is necessary to make important medical decisions and then act upon them in a short course for emergency medical technicians. It takes seven years to become a lawyer, but we accept legal advice from friends, self-help books, and the Internet. Student-teachers instruct at the primary and secondary level. And teenage military personnel control our fate. Perhaps the only occupation in which unequivocal certification is required is commercial airline pilot. One does not often see an apprentice at the controls of a 747. The more one knows, the easier it is to locate the requested material; thus, the truly knowledgeable person makes the best reference worker. But the specialized or difficult query only presents itself occasionally. It is a sad truth, but one that only the obdurate would deny: Most questions are easy, repetitive, or directional. Nevertheless, these simple queries require servicing too.

A Service Ethic

Librarianship is a service profession and reference is the nexus to which knowledge and materials flow and from which help emanates. Each year individual reference personnel are bombarded with thousands of problems, most of which are easily solved. For some inexplicable reason, these curious, knowledgeable, and motivated people cannot seem to answer the queries correctly. Perhaps the research indicating that only 55 percent of tendered questions are answered correctly (Hernon & McClure, 1986) is flawed, but no one has proven a higher percentage.

If this assessment is correct, it is an extremely negative reflection on the work that we are doing. No other profession would accept almost 50 failures out of every 100 attempts—whether in court, the operating theater, or the classroom. Perhaps information professionals do not take their tasks seriously enough. If reference workers think that questions are insignificant and thus fail to provide adequate or accurate responses, then patrons may suspect that their needs really are unimportant, a perspective they often indicate by commencing with phrases such as, "I'm sorry to bother you, but I have a really stupid question." These two attitudes reinforce each other. Although this cycle of irresponsible and inaccurate

---

Ethical Reference Service

1. Serve all patrons equally and objectively.
2. Do not allow personal commitments to intrude.
3. Do not sacrifice everything for the sake of information provision.
4. Avoid conflicts of interest.
5. Protect privacy and confidentiality.
6. Protect your employer's investments.
7. Cultivate a service ethic.
8. Market your availability and willingness to help.
9. Provide added value.
10. Recreate yourself as an indispensable provider of whatever is required.

replies was hardly acceptable ten years ago, there was no real alternative for the public or academic information seeker.

Today, things are very different: Almost anyone in the developed countries and many people in the Third World have some access to networked computers that offer a host of sophisticated search engines, each of which can scour the Internet extremely quickly and provide websites that either answer questions or lead to viable sources. Shoddy responses will put us out of business. To understand the serious nature of our service failures, one need only contrast the success rate of the medical profession. It is certainly possible for a doctor to discover that a patient has an incurable disease or for a surgeon to lose someone during an operation. But for every such failure, hundreds of thousands of medical information seekers visit their doctors, who after cursory examinations tender some well-received advice and a prescription for a miracle drug. The patient goes home believing that the remedy really does affect the cold, flu, or pain, even though there is often no valid correlation between the doctor's services and the alteration in the patient's condition. The difference here is that the information seeker apparently failed with the librarian and succeeded with the doctor. What this seems to mean is that we are ethically constrained to improve our attitude, service commitment, and accuracy rate or we should close down the reference desk and find other occupations.

Traditional Issues

We continue to face the same challenges that have haunted us for more than a century, but because of changes in technology, the ethos, and the global context, these same problems are much exacerbated. Objective information provision, conflict of interest, confidentiality, dishonesty, and protection of minors concerned information disseminators in 1900, in 1950, and still today, when these issues continue to challenge especially those whose ethical commitments create dilemmas, where others are able to act unthinkingly. Forty years ago, D. J. Foskett (1962) insisted that librarians' personal beliefs—concerning politics, religion, and morals, for example—must never intrude in their professional service; personal ethics must never influence the way in which we guide patrons, offer advice, evaluate materials, or provide information. This stubbornly unrealistic attitude, though based on good intentions, and similar to ethical strictures in other professions, results in bizarrely untenable situations. Thus, as journalists who want to protect their sources are sometimes jailed, as lawyers who refuse to defend an admitted serial killer may be disbarred, as priests who attempt to ameliorate social conditions in Third World countries are often criticized, as doctors who refuse to perform some medical procedures might be sanctioned, so too are librarians castigated or even fired for refusing to aid and abet dishonest activity or grievous harm. John Swan (Wiener, 1987) insisted that information disseminators are not privy to patrons' intentions and that people have the right to read and make up their own minds on all issues. This is sensible and tenable, but not always applicable. A reference librarian at a major research facility told me that a student requested help in creating references to a series of nonexistent sources, since he had merely copied his essay directly from a single text. She insisted that it was her duty to help, which she did. When I asked her how she would feel if her 14 year old son did the same thing, she was taken aback. At a lecture I presented to some hundred participants, I wondered how reference personnel would react if asked by an abuser for the address of the shelter where his wife and children had taken refuge. Some audience members indicated that they would not help. An individual leaning against the back wall concluded the discussion by observing that he was the head of the entire district's library system and that if he discovered that any of his employees had refused to help a patron, he would fire him or her. When I asked him if he would locate the shelter's address for the hypothetical abuser, he replied that he would not!

There is no doubt that the intrusion of every individual's personal perspective into the rendering of reference aid would result in chaos. Legal and medical reference workers frequently provide information that may have extremely deleterious results, effects that the person believes are unethical, but he or she would be of little help if every emergency request that a lawyer or doctor made was first analyzed in terms of potential consequences. Nevertheless, although we must have a strong and abiding commitment to information provision, we are also members of society and we may not cause harm to others because some tenuous professional edict insists that we act as if we were information-dispensing automatons. If there is any characteristic that differentiates professionals from laypersons, it is the necessity to consider our actions and to proceed in an accountable manner. After many years of adverse reaction to this point of view, other scholars are now willing to reject the duality that is mandated in the seventh principle of the ALA Code of Ethics. For example, Thomas Froehlich (1992) observes that respect for self requires that we affirm our personal opinions, which should not be mitigated in an attempt to achieve objectivity. He believes that the ALA position promotes schizophrenia and ambiguity. An even stronger position is taken by Elizabeth Irish (1992), who insists that "There are occasions when personal beliefs and societal concerns arise which conflict with the code. In these instances, the librarian should follow the higher ethical standard" (p. 14).

It is obvious that in librarianship, conflicts of interest do not present a major obstacle to living the ethical life. The possibility of swaying an employee's decision to purchase or subscribe to material, lease a data base, or contract for an expensive system is minimal. Misconduct of this nature may infrequently occur, but there is very little opportunity for conflict in the reference arena. A wise person would distance him or herself from even the faintest suspicion that a conflict of interest exists, by, for example, refusing all gifts, even if offered after the fact, say, once an expensive purchase has been finalized.

Reference service is one of the few professional interactions that takes place in a public forum. Dozens of people may be in the area and overhear the exchange. And although these queries are not usually sensitive and it is often feasible to move to a more secluded location or a private office, very few patrons or librarians avail themselves of this possibility. Most people do not care if their privacy is invaded. Nevertheless, we should make every effort to interact in a circumspect manner, help in confidence, and protect the informational interchange from colleagues, staff, and administrators as well as from the patron's relatives, friends, instructors, parole officers, and anyone else who wants to know what a person is doing, seeking, or reading.

Confidentiality is the mark of a true service professional. Plumbers, electricians, or masons do not mind discussing their day's work with loved ones, and it is improbable that unions or contractors would balk should they discover that a bricklayer spent the evening describing the intricate pattern he had created on the 58th floor of a Chicago skyscraper. But doctors, lawyers, and clergy keep their thoughts to themselves. If they share professional intimacies with others, and this abrogation is discovered, they may be sanctioned or even lose their positions.

All of this is clear, and yet nurses or clerks leave files out in the open; pharmacists demand personal data from prescription seekers while a gaggle of customers eavesdrop; and doctors converse with the ailing in rooms whose paper-thin walls allow every medical privation to ripple through a waiting patient's consciousness. In addition to protecting oral confidences, reference personnel should secrete hard copy and encrypt electronic records, data, online searches, or anything else that might link a patron and his or her informational needs. Leaving material on a counter or an open computer for anyone to peruse is as unethical as broadcasting the names and reading habits of patrons on the college radio station.

Dishonesty is far more prevalent among patrons, especially students, than it is in the professional arena. Most reference librarians are honest and caring providers. Even those whose ethical commitment is questionable have little opportunity to steal or embezzle from their employers or harm patrons. Library users, on the other hand, may threaten physical harm, abuse privileges, refuse to return materials, or appropriate data and information and pass it off as their own in both the business and academic environments. Reference librarians are not in the position to deduce usage or application from a request, but whenever they strongly suspect and especially when they have apodictic knowledge that some major harm will ensue, they must refuse to cooperate. This position, which I have advocated for more than a quarter of a century, is not censorship nor can it be construed as such.

It is simply a human refusal to aid and abet an unethical act or the commission of a crime. In schools or at a college or university, students are taught and constantly reminded that plagiary is unacceptable and may have devastating consequences. Even where honor codes presumably control students' bad intentions, dishonest activity occurs, often with astonishing frequency. It is generally believed that about 70 percent of all students cheat in some way. Reference librarians are not trained to police nor should they do so, but they must also avoid helping the dishonest. On the other hand, when the inevitable occurs and an instructor shows up searching for proof that a student has plagiarized a paper, we must never reveal what we know. This places us in a most peculiar and uncomfortable position, but I see no alternative: If we are to affirm the social contract, we cannot abet dishonesty and if we wish to protect the sanctity of the informational exchange, we must not break confidence. We lose no matter what we do. We also gain, by affirming principled necessity, despite the sometimes awkward consequences.

Minors, and especially very young children, are different from adults. They are immature, have different social and legal obligations, and are therefore treated differently by individuals, the courts, and society. In the library environment, they are generally given their own areas with appropriate materials. If a legally responsible guardian gives permission, then they may use or check out anything they desire. Many librarians believe that children should be treated differently. The ALA position is that age is not a determining factor; and some scholars, for example, Joan Kennedy Taylor (1997), insist that librarians should not protect minors from themselves by abridging their Constitutional rights, an action that is typically approbated by most unthinking people.

Technological Complications

During the 1970s, the first public computers arrived in libraries. These dumb terminals gave access to often incomplete library holdings, since retrospective conversion projects had yet to take place. It was also possible to do a mediated search on a limited number of data bases, collected and mounted by vendors such as Dialog. The librarian interviewed the patron, did the search in private, and presented the offprint some days later. As the years went by, additional public electronic access was provided including OCLC and RLIN terminals and eventually user-friendly interfaces that allowed patrons to do unmediated searches on Dialog, BRS, and other systems. A host of sometimes short-lived technologies followed including improvements in microformats, COM reader-printers, computer indexes with full-text contained in a large cassette collection, and CD-ROMS. Each of these developments increased the possibility for ethical infractions for both publishers and patrons. For example, in an attempt to get the early technological indexes to market as quickly as possible, accuracy was sacrificed for speed. The error rate was far too high and many users were frustrated when they could not locate the cited material. Patrons who had the freedom to search on their own and print without cost might configure a computer to reproduce 50 annual reports and then walk away. The paper waste was excessive. No wonder administrators instituted printing charges.

Despite what appears to be an extraordinary amount of technological activity, reference work remained fairly consistent. Although some patrons made excellent use of the available technology, traditional resources were still emphasized, and many people avoided computers and other devices. The major change occurred when the Internet became user friendly, when browsers made gophers obsolete, and search engines allowed one to locate precisely what was required using a graphic interface. Once this occurred, libraries began to mount their catalogues on the Internet, journals began to appear in electronic format, and the indexing companies switched to Internet access. In just a few years, some important general indexes dramatically increased the number of full-text documents available, and users could not resist what was offered. Now external, online access to hundreds of superb, discipline-specific data bases makes it possible for any authenticated user to do sophisticated research (at least for some proscribed chronological periods) without leaving home. The additional possibilities laid out in millions of replete World Wide Web pages only confirms the aficionado in his or her unwarranted belief that everything is available in convenient digital format at any connected monitor.

The ethos of research has changed so dramatically that it would be impossible to reacculturate younger people to the traditional demands and necessities of scholarly endeavor. Without scrupulous tutelage and stringent pedagogical requirements, students and subsequently the next generation of scholars will limit themselves to whatever is conveniently at hand. It is certainly unethical to settle for an abstract when the article is not available in full-text, or to choose just what happens to appear on the screen, even though it is not as pertinent as another essay whose access requires a trip to the library or to the microfiche reader. Most people do not realize that the smaller data bases only index two or three thousand periodicals. *Ingenta*, one of the largest, includes 26,000 magazines and journals and this is certainly an impressively substantial number, but when one considers that there are 500,000 serials published in the world, and that Harvard subscribes to more than 100,000, this 26,000 does not cover the full gamut of the specific discipline an upper division undergraduate, graduate, or scholar may require. That is why there are specialized data bases for biology, chemistry, literature, music, and hundreds of other areas, but generally these only offer citations and abstracts. When the full text is unavailable online, the researcher must avoid the temptation to fragment knowledge. Convenience is but one factor we should use to make scholarly decisions.

Unfiltered access to the Internet presents some major ethical challenges even to those whose commitment to intellectual freedom is unequivocal. There is nothing we can do about material accessed at home, but using the Internet to locate legal or health advice or pornography, fulfill assignments, purchase drugs without a prescription, gamble, hack or crack, or perpetrate crimes in a public facility presents insurmountable problems. If patrons work on their own and there are no complaints, reference librarians should leave them alone. Monitoring and controlling even students in primary and secondary school media centers is offensive to those who defend intellectual freedom. It is not our business to mediate between users and the virtual world. On the other hand, if someone requests help, then it is incumbent on professionals to share their knowledge. Thus, one might observe that many web pages contain misleading, false, or harmful information. This would be especially useful advice if someone were searching for a cure for some ghastly ailment. Every person accessing legal information may not realize that following a path laid out in an advice column could lead to contempt of court or prison. In these cases, we are merely indicating that the material on the Internet can be unreliable, and it is up to the user to learn to evaluate sources. As for pornography, the most controversial issue in information provision in a public forum, I take the unequivocal hard line: it is none of our business what a person is doing as long as he or she is civil and not annoying others. People who unfairly claim that a naked image on a distant computer screen produces a hostile environment or constitutes sexual harassment would be surprised to learn that political, blasphemous, or violent texts and images would have the same effect on others. In a democracy, it is unacceptable for the minority to control the majority. The courts generally agree. Finally, it is obvious that a patron hacking, cracking, or perpetrating a crime has crossed a boundary; we do not have control over judicial matters. Depending on the circumstances, if we become aware of such wrongdoing, we should request that the patron desist or contact the appropriate authorities including supervisors, administrators, or the police.

Changes in Reference Work

Librarians who work in the public sector sometimes hold two graduate degrees; those in special collections may have advanced degrees in law or the health related professions; and many faculty members in academic institutions have doctorates. I wonder whether it is ethical to pay these people substantial salaries and then have them spend their time instructing patrons in rudimentary searching techniques, directing people to various locations, rebooting computers, deleting inappropriate material from monitors, changing toner cartridges, reloading printers with paper, making technical adjustments to computers, printers, servers, and other devices, or otherwise performing petty tasks better left to paraprofessionals or technicians.

Just 15 or 20 years ago, most of our time was spent helping people locate sources or information, doing research or online searches, and advising patrons concerning collections, tools, or methodologies. Today, a high percentage of any reference worker's time is allocated to non-intellectual tasks. This is wasteful and should be depressing for anyone who gives it any consideration. Instead, we have fully accepted our new situation. We defend what we do and then spend our off-desk time surfing the Internet, reading thousands of superfluous email messages (from people, who in the past, would never have bothered to write anything to anyone), participating in banal listerv discussions, or creating Web pages that are essentially duplicated hundreds of times on other libraries' sites.

We could be doing things differently. That is why Keith Ewing and I (1995) offered the readers of a *Journal of Academic Librarianship* symposium the opportunity to consider the elimination of reference. We purposely presented this iconoclastic position in order to stimulate respondents to reconsider what we are doing. One of the unstated implications of our conjectures is that it is unethical to waste an employer's money. Technological innovations that allow sophisticated external searching across a broad spectrum of sometimes full-text files have already created a disintermediated environment, one in which only novices and the confused seek basic help. As the children of the computer generation mature, they will become extremely proficient at locating materials and will no longer require reference guidance, instruction, or advice. To continue to insist that sophisticated and esoteric research services are required in the face of overwhelming evidence to the contrary, to present tangential or distorted arguments in order to protect our image or our positions, to refuse to change with the times, is to act unprofessionally and unethically. Librarians have been strong defenders of technological innovation, but the mere implementation of technological devices that improve access to information is inadequate. Indeed, it is the very application of this technology that has resulted in the new ethos.

It would not be very difficult to truly revise and restructure reference, offering our substantive expertise where it is needed and concomitantly addressing the primary but simplistic needs of most on-site patrons differently. Tiered, roaming, telephonic, online, video, off-site, and fuller research service, rather than mere guidance, provide alternatives to the traditional sedentary librarian. That there is a need for this is confirmed by the new approach to information provision taken by Questia, a commercial firm that charges a monthly fee and then provides services to those who subscribe. It hardly seems credible that students would contact a company and pay for documents when it is possible to have their needs met by a reference librarian, one who is frequently happy to help someone located thousands of miles away — at another school, in another state, even in another country. We are called upon so infrequently for serious consultation because people do not realize that we are available, because people are shy and do not want to impose upon us, and because we do not offer the immediate provision of precisely what the patron requires. What we must do in order to maintain our professional position is to market our skills and improve our services. This does not mean that we should provide a complete market analysis for a company or write research papers for students. It does mean that to fulfill our potential and to accommodate the new environment presented to us by the information age, we must rethink, reconfigure, and restructure. To act otherwise is to follow the easy but unethical road taken so frequently by others. With some small but significant adjustments we can protect our honor and dignity, truly provide for those who require help, and avoid becoming functional anachronisms.

Information Malpractice

Supermarket tabloids, the Internet, and librarians all tender information. The difference is that no one expectats sensationalist newspapers or web sites to provide reliable, valid, or truthful material. Some of what they proffer reflects reality, some of it is inadvertently distorted, and some is unequivocally false. Professionals who help locate information are approached because the patron has an implicit belief that the librarian is knowledgeable and trustworthy and will provide appropriate guidance and valid material. When this trust is unfulfilled, users are disappointed, frustrated, and hurt. In contractual situations, e.g., when a lawyer or doctor causes harm, clients or patients sue. So may library patrons, although this occurs extremely rarely. Nevertheless, there is a burgeoning body of literature on misinformation provision, information malpractice, and the legal liabilities we may incur. Early remarks by Allan Angoff (1976), Anne Mintz (1985), and Robert Hauptman (1988), *inter alios,* were followed by fuller and sometimes extremely detailed examinations during the 1990s, including analyses by Pamela Samuelson (1993), Marianne Puckett and James Pat Craig (1993), and Stuart Ferguson and John Weckert (1998). All commentators on the subject take the possibility of legal action seriously, although their emphases are colored by their viewpoints. Some approach malpractice actions from a purely legal perspective; others are more interested in a broader, ethical understanding of the etiology and effects of misinformation in relation to the possibility of liability claims. The simple conclusion to be drawn from all of this discussion is that although malpractice suits are not as frequent as some of us thought they would be, there is still much to be feared here as we develop and evolve in the information age. To avoid an epidemic of actions, general reference personnel must always endeavor to provide accurate information and guidance. As noted above, tendering correct answers 55 percent of the time is a professional outrage, an anomaly that could help to sway a judge and jury to favor a plaintiff claiming information harm.

Librarians, acting as intermediaries, answering specific questions based on data contained in various sources, offering explanations and advice, i.e., providing information, may be liable for misinforming a patron who subsequently suffers some harm. Ferguson and Weckert (1998) discuss six germane cases in some detail, the first of which occurred in 1969. These cases confirm the authors' contention that the ethos in which we operate has changed; additionally, they cite John Levett's belief "that the reference librarian is no longer seen as 'a passive, non-thinking, non-judging, non-evaluating dispenser of neutral, value-free information whose origins and quality lie beyond her purview.'" We are professionals, responsible and accountable for our actions.

Unmediated information also presents a challenge. Samuelson (1993) differentiates between printed and electronic sources. The former type of material is protected and the courts have usually, though not always, favored publishers, librarians, and even authors over suitors who claimed that a printed text misled and thus harmed them. Electronic information is different, because of its technological nature, because software cannot be inspected prior to purchase, and because software does a task that the reader of an instructing book usually performs. And so here, according to Samuelson, lies the possibility for major legal problems. Electronic misinformation published by commercial firms or professional organizations and offered by librarians on publicly accessible data bases is only a metaphorical step away from the purchasable software to which Samuleson refers.

Ronglin Wan (1994) suggests that insurance, contractual agreements, disclaimers, avoidance of advice, updating collections, consultations with colleagues, and competence can help to protect against legal actions. Sadly, there are problems with most of these strategies. For example, although some librarians are provided with liability insurance or legal indemnification by their employers, most information workers do not take the possibility of a suit seriously enough to consider insuring against it, and even if they did, they would hesitate to undertake the payment of ongoing premiums. Disclaimers indicate to patrons that they must assume responsibility for validating data and information, but courts do not look favorably on disclaimers when the defendant is negligent. Refusing to offer advice out of fear is a service failure; additionally, we might be sued for misleading the public, since we purposely held back information that might have helped a person make a judicious decision. Finally, an updated collection is a reasonable expectation on the part of the user; and weeding out superceded materials is part of any collection management program, and although some iconoclasts insist that librarians should help to control the validity of the literature, most commentators believe that culling materials that ostensibly are misleading or untrue (bizarre medical advice, questionable legal tactics, astrological tracts, religious gibberish) amounts to censorship. Nevertheless, Wan's suggestions should be borne in mind as we attempt to offer ethical information provision, while concomitantly protecting ourselves from legal actions.

A Misleading Solution

In 1991, Gillian Gremmels published an incisive essay in which she suggests that some of the typical ethical dilemmas that we face can be

---

Case Study: The President Needs Immediate Help

Kim Minto is diversely knowledgeable in all disciplines. Indeed, he was selected to appear on two television game shows where real knowledge is a prerequisite. Lamentably, he was so nervous that he won very little money. Minto is also an extraordinarily dedicated and caring reference professional. He almost never gives up, follows leads, calls and contacts people, and stays with a problem until the patron is satisfied with the answer. These tough queries only occur occasionally and most of Minto's time is spent coddling young college undergraduates whose traditional and electronic research skills are surprisingly underdeveloped.

On an unusually busy Friday afternoon, he had just begun helping two patrons with some complex queries. The first needed an explanation concerning business norms and the second had to locate six refereed articles on the reason that pharmacological treatment has replaced psychotherapy. The phone rang: It was the president of the university and he needed some statistics immediately. He wondered whether Minto could call him back within three minutes. Otherwise, the information would be of no use.

---

solved by adopting a new structuring principle for helping patrons. In those situations that seem to warrant ethical consideration and thus the possibility of refusing a request for help, we should consider the broader social context, rather than the individual user's needs. Gremmels insists that the reference worker is not a value-free, objective automaton. He or she does not merely accept a query and provide a predetermined response; rather, the librarian, the patron, and the tools all work together to produce an answer. For Gremmels, considering society's needs results in the following reoriented advantages: there are no easy solutions; we are neither neutral nor objective; we can serve the public interest; we are able to turn away potentially harmful inquiries; and we are able to do more. What all of this means is that the individual is asked to sacrifice something for the good of society. In a political context, depending on details, this would be called socialism or communism. Gremmels uses communitarianism, a less offensive locution favored by the sociologist Amitai Etzioni, but which has the same unpleasant characteristic: it subverts individuality and insists that individuals make sacrifices for the good of the general populace. Conservatives find this reprehensible and even liberals balk at the lack of free choice this entails. Therefore, Gremmels's solution would not be acceptable to many practitioners. Two years after her piece appeared, Bradley Chilton (1993) affirmed her position. He argues that the public interest ethic takes precedence over individual needs. Librarians are accountable not only to the information seeker but also to the community. He believes that by applying the public interest ethic we would "inject responsibility and wisdom back into the practice of librarianship" (p. 50). Gremmels and Chilton defend a hyperbolic version of the perspective I laid out a quarter of a century ago (Hauptman, 1976). But I only mean to allow information professionals the freedom to think and act according to their conscience by considering potential social harm. I do not advocate the devaluation of individual rights or needs in favor of a nebulous social good. Communitarian possibilities are superficially seductive but detrimental because they abrogate the personal rights and liberties that characterize a democracy. Sacrifices must be freely chosen, not coerced. Gremmels and Chilton trick us.

7

· · · · · · · · · · · · ·

Special Libraries

The correctness of actions taken by medical practitioners does not vary across specializations. Opthalmologists do not act in one way and endocrinologists in another. If it is unacceptable for one of these doctors to file false reports in order to increase personal revenues from Medicaid, then it is equally unethical for the other to do so. Oncologists may not purposely deceive patients, even for their own good (although they sometimes do so), and neither may cardiologists. Thus, it is a reasonable assumption that the same situation would apply in other professions. Even an experienced librarian might expect that ethical commitment, correct action, and unacceptable behavior would be fairly consistent across the various specializations. As it turns out though, he or she would be surprisingly disappointed. Librarians who specialize in legal, medical, or corporate information control operate in diverse cultural environments, adhere to very different legal and ethical mandates, and are proscribed from disseminating specific types of information to specific types of patrons. At first glance, this appears to be totally unacceptable: a fluctuating ethic depending upon a given situation hardly warrants serious consideration; its flexibility renders it otiose. Once one scrutinizes the unusual circumstances, however, most practitioners are easily convinced that there are valid reasons for operating in this bizarre fashion. But it is also possible to view all of these convoluted and legalistic arguments from the cynical position that some sociologists take in relation to all professional

---

Special Ethics

1. Do not provide legal advice or interpretation.
2. Do not provide medical advice or interpretation.
3. Do not harm the corporation at which you work.
4. The environment must determine your actions.
5. The principles, beliefs, rules, and regulations that generally control the storage, access, retrieval, and dissemination of data and information may be altered, skewed, or distorted for a variety of sometimes illegitimate or self-serving reasons.

---

groups: we are less interested in protecting the patron than we are in ensuring that information is not easily accessible without professional consultation, which would decrease the income stream; that neither organizations nor individuals will be sued for information malpractice; or that nothing is done to harm the corporation.

The ethical problems that arise in special libraries vary dramatically depending on whether one is dealing with legal, medical, or corporate requests, whether the patron is a layperson or a lawyer or doctor, whether the individual is affiliated with the library's organization, and whether the information is crucial, confidential, proprietary, or potentially harmful — to uninformed individuals, employees, or the organization itself. Sometimes a conflict exists between two commitments or obligations and the unpleasant result is that ancillary concerns take precedence over true ethical choices.

The Law

Law libraries or collections come in many different forms: large law firms may have first-class libraries and one or more full-time librarians; individual law firms also have access to consortial collections; county, state, and other governmental entities may fund excellent, fully-staffed libraries; law schools serve their primary clientele through replete collections, online services, and librarians who generally hold JDs; and academic and public libraries may maintain collections and offer legal reference. Even some of the specialized libraries are open to the public and provide various services including use of serials and monographs as well as reference aid. If a person in need of legal advice could visit a real or virtual collection, consult with a reference librarian, and come away equipped to triumph in court, lawyers would lose an increasingly large percentage of their business. In order to protect themselves from this sobering possibility, they have had laws passed that make it illegal to tender legal advice without a license, which obviously makes it impossible for a layperson to explain some intricate aspect of the law to an unsophisticated, indigent, illiterate, or deranged patron. Ironically, even a credentialed lawyer working in an academic library may not offer advice. Lawyers are so adamant that people should avoid *pro se* entanglements that they have tried to control and censor self-help materials by pressuring or suing publishers like Nolo Press; naturally, the First Amendment protects those who wish to disseminate legal information.

Nevertheless, the law is a harsh mistress, and those in a position to offer legal advice generally will refuse to do so because it is illegal. This does not mean that it is unethical, but because fear, habitual adherence to the law, and eventual enculturization are such strong modifiers of both physical and mental behavior, we have come to believe that it is unethical to offer legal advice regardless of type, substance, sensitivity, importance, situation, or necessity. We may point to the annotated state statutes or the legal sections of Lexis-Nexis; we may teach someone how a tool works or how to read a legal citation; we may even indicate that a law encyclopedia is more appropriate than *Black's Law Dictionary* in a given case, but we are fully and threateningly proscribed from more clearly defining a term or explaining the complexities of some esoteric ordinance, statute, or case. This, we are told, is because we have not been initiated into the subtleties that only credentialed members of the bar can fully understand and so we may mislead or harm a naive patron. And this could lead to a lawsuit. Then why are exceptions not made for lawyers who work in academic libraries? Why would a signed disclaimer from a desperate person not cover the aforementioned contingency? And why is it that librarians constantly add value by offering additional help, information, and advice concerning copyright, graduate schools, psychology, bioethics, literary reputations, and thousands of other equally sensitive and important matters, but when it comes to the law, we draw an uncrossable line?

Most commentators agree with the RUSA Guidelines (2000), which insist that librarians should not interpret nor evaluate legal information. Maria Protti (1991) argues that law librarians should tender useful information, maintain confidentiality, and, iconoclastically, have more flexibility in interpreting the law. Since we have the right to defend ourselves in court, we logically have the right to the information that will allow us to do the job well enough to convince a judge and jury that we understand the relevant law. We must be able to make a tenable case; we must be able to stand a chance of proving that we are correct. If law (and other) librarians are proscribed or hindered from fully helping us, while the opposition has these advantages from their own advanced training as well as the advice and interpretive remarks of colleagues, then the *pro se* litigant or defendant is placed at a distinct disadvantage. Protti (1991) concludes, "Law librarians are increasingly called upon to explain, distinguish, and find judicial opinions, statutes, and rules" (p. 242).

Perhaps it is time to rethink the traditional position, especially since it derives from self-protection. Pat Lorenzo (1995) notes that it is often difficult to distinguish between assistance and advice. This raises the fear of liability suits, which in turn may diminish the service provided to the patron. This situation obtains in law collections, where the librarian may be a member of the bar, and especially in the public and academic environment, where the information generalist may know virtually nothing about the law and its labyrinthine complexities, where the collection is inadequate or outmoded, and where people are confused and frustrated.

The introduction of the Lexis-Nexis database into public and academic libraries has dramatically altered the way in which legal research is done. Now an untutored layperson or high school student is able to locate apposite statutory and case law in any venue by simply typing key words into appropriate search boxes. The system is admittedly complicated and a user must learn where to go, how to enter terms, and what to choose, but there is no doubt that Lexis-Nexis empowers a user with legal research skills that used to take years to master. It also makes the broad federal and state legal mandates available at a single keyboard; one does not have to travel to a specialized collection to locate the Delaware or Alaska state statutes. But patrons may not know what to do with the vast quantities of text that scroll by. They may not know what is relevant or useful, since they usually cannot even distinguish among the different types of law and do not know whether a municipal ordinance, a state statute, or a federal law takes precedence in a given situation. They cannot effectively proceed with their real or hypothetical (academic) case if they do not understand the terminology or the conventions, rules, regulations, and constraints under which judges, juries, and lawyers operate. In *The Trial*, Franz Kafka's (1984) protagonist had a very difficult time ferreting out the information that could have saved his life. Ironically, here we have far too much information and it beclouds the issue in the same way that too little hinders. It is precisely at this point that the librarian traditionally steps in to help patrons, but since it is illegal and ostensibly unethical to advise, interpret, or evaluate, patrons either stumble through on their own or hire an attorney (which is not a viable option for a student doing a report). Allowing someone (especially in an academic setting) to leave in a state of confusion is what is unethical.

A more unusual environment, which some administrators believe warrants special conditions (censorship, for example), is found in the asylum and especially the prison library, where many of the incarcerated turn to a study of the law to further their chances of release. A long-serving librarian, even one with no legal training, undoubtedly acquires much useful knowledge during the course of his or her career. It is ostensibly unethical to share this knowledge with these people for the reasons noted above; in these cases, though, the inmates have no other recourse. They cannot try another facility or collection; they cannot easily consult a lawyer, since they are limited to the physical environs of the institution. The best they can do is a brief telephone call or a website or chatroom, which may truly provide misleading information. Karen Westwood (1994) informs us that when a prisoner enters the law library at a maximum security prison where she serves, he only has ten minutes to discuss matters with her. Then she returns to her home library and does the research. She does not offer advice and she protects her patrons' confidences. This is helpful, but it may not be enough.

It is necessary to insist that I am not arguing for the broad dissemination of legal advice, interpretation, and evaluation by neophytes, amateurs, or self-proclaimed but uncredentialed legal experts. What I am attempting here is to differentiate legal demands imposed by self-protecting professionals from mandates that derive from some real ethical necessity or obligation.

Medicine

Medical and legal librarianship have much in common: they are oriented and controlled by the same impulses and necessities; they maintain the same proscriptions against tendering advice and interpreting professional esoterica, and they serve credentialed practitioners with care and diligence, at times offering life-saving information, while concomitantly shortchanging the very people who really require their assistance. In a number of obvious ways, medical information is more crucial than legal materials, since a person's degenerating health sometimes requires immediate attention, whereas legal machinations may continue for many years. In some venues, it is not unusual for a case to drag on for decades or even across generations, as Charles Dickens (1966) agonizingly shows in *Bleak House*.

A person who is having an adverse reaction to a necessary drug may wish to look at the *Physicians' Desk Reference* in order to discover whether she should make some changes. If she is unable to understand a term or locution and asks for help, it is disconcerting to hear that she should consult a doctor. Perhaps she is deathly afraid of doctors or cannot afford frequent visits (which can run to $100 for a brief consultation). She might be illiterate and require an oral articulation; she might ask a question concerning a noted dosage or side effect. According to both legal and concomitant ethical mandates, many of these simple requests must be met with silence. As in other critical situations, when the misapplication of information can cause harm, which may additionally result in malpractice suits, medical librarians must adhere to a precise agenda when helping patrons or answering queries. This position is theoretically and pragmatically understandable and defensible, but it raises the same questions that occur in legal librarianship: are we really interested in protecting patrons or patients or is this merely a tack on the part of the medical community to further its own interests, and do librarians cooperate in order to make certain that we do not end up at the wrong end of a malpractice suit?

If indicating to patrons that 'ligament' and 'muscle' are two different parts of the body or that 'gram' and 'ounce' do not precisely coincide constitutes unethical activity, why is it that untutored high school graduates who work as clerks in health food stores may dispense vast quantities of erroneous and harmful information concerning vitamins, supplements, and other pills that people ingest sometimes to their extreme detriment? It is illegal to practice medicine without a license, but it is not necessarily unethical: A practitioner with 25 years of superb service may be jailed when it is discovered that he is not really a certified doctor, and this despite the howls of protest from the thousands of patients he has helped, cured, or succored over the course of his long career. We are not truly interested in knowledge, ability, or competence; the critical point here is a legalism founded upon the need for professional self-preservation.

There is a surprisingly replete body of literature on the ethical aspects of medical librarianship. Much of it is repetitive and uninspired. The traditional conservative approach to information dissemination is tediously repeated and despite some cosmetic changes, recent work differs very little from Helen Crawford's (1978) position, which she articulated almost a quarter of a century ago: "We are uncomfortable with patients and their relatives and with laymen in general, uneasy at intruding upon the doctor-patient relationship, and fearful of doing harm" (p. 336). Here, I contradict my own position in *Ethical Challenges in Librarianship* (Hauptman, 1988), which is too forgiving. As information professionals, we may desire to dispense what is requested but we are shackled by law and derivative ethical commitments that may be as harmful in their own inflexibility as the misinformation they attempt to stifle. M. Sandra Wood (1991), in a comprehensive overview of ethics in health sciences libraries, touches upon many of the same issues that concern law librarians including access, quality, confidentiality, and liability. She points out that timely and accurate information is crucial since a physician or surgeon may succeed or fail depending on the speed of provision and integrity of the material. Public, academic, bio-medical, hospital, and patient libraries might collect germane material and offer access to appropriate data bases. Unless admittance is proscribed because it is a private institution or because patients are barred from a hospital library maintained exclusively for physicians, anyone may enter and use a computer or browse the stacks. Ethical problems arise when the surgeon is treated differently than the pregnant teenager. As Wood (1991) observes, library policy may severely delimit service depending on patron status. That consumer health information libraries or collections are now commonplace does not alter the fact that information specialists are constrained legally and ethically from providing medical advice to patrons.

Nancy Rainey (1988) describes a policy that exacerbates this by creating an unwieldy patron taxonomy for a pharmaceutical library that dispenses drug information: primary users (faculty and graduate students) get complete service; secondary patrons (undergraduates) do not require drug data; community pharmacists receive full service; non–health care professionals get minimal drug information; and laypersons are not helped. The librarians, we are told, do have a responsibility to tender information, but this must be counterbalanced by the need to protect patrons from potentially harmful or liability-producing material. The literature of the last 25 years is replete with countless articles that insist that information professionals must not function in *loco parentis;* they must not control the flow of information at their personal discretion even to protect the vulnerable; and they must not censor. Apparently drug data is an exception, and the ethical contradictions do not appear to bother Rainey and her colleagues.

In the United Kingdom, medical practitioners who fail to provide adequate or accurate information are subject to liability suits (Gann, 1995). Although medical librarians and many consumer health information service professionals are not certified doctors, the information they provide or fail to offer can have a significant effect on the patron's health. This is true in the United States as well, where some people may derive their health information from materials housed or accessed in public facilities; the only intermediary may be a librarian. The situation is similar in South Africa (van Tonder, 1994), where patients have the right to all information available so that they can make the best decision concerning their condition and treatment. Here, as in most Western countries, withholding crucial information against the patient's will does occasionally occur, but the implication is that this is unusual. In Japan, however, doctors routinely distort, dissimulate, and lie to patients to protect them from bad news. It is a fair deduction that medical librarians in Japan would be under no ethical constraint to subvert this trend.

A courageous attempt to counter the conservative perspective discussed above can be found in "Abandoning the Comfort Zone" (1994). The anonymous author argues that things <u>are</u> different now because collections have grown, public libraries purchase many medical and health related items, and some scholars advocate dispensing medical information rather than withholding it. The author insists that librarians must be held accountable for the information offered. Although he briefly calls into question limited telephone help as well as proscriptions that preclude interpretation, his treatise includes the admonition to "Distinguish between information and advice." The six other concluding points (e.g., interview carefully, refer, train) do not alter matters in any appreciable way. And one iconoclastic call to arms is not enough to alter the *Zeitgeist*.

Business

Corporate collections and their professional librarians are different and they operate under different mandates, what Jean Preer (1991) terms special ethics for special librarians. These collections exist to serve the company, whose *raison d'être* or pecuniary obligation is to produce a profit for the owners or stockholders. Thus, the public may be barred from entering and telephone inquires are probably rejected, since the caller may be a competitive intelligence operative attempting in some subtle fashion to wheedle data or information from the naive or ethically cooperative information officer. Professional librarians who work in a corporate setting have to enculturate themselves to a totally new ethos, one in which information is not only not free, but rather proprietary, proscribed, confidential, scrupulously protected, and more highly valued than the physical means of production or even the final product. The secret formulas for Coca-Cola and Kentucky Fried Chicken are metaphoric reminders of just how valuable basic information can be. Additionally, the American business community has only belatedly come to recognize the value of an ethical commitment to some higher standard than the bottom line. Profit is still the single most important goal but at least now employee rights, social responsibility, philanthropy, and other secondary objectives are recognized and nurtured. But we are still in a transitional period and many of the business world's top executives never had a course in ethics, were never

---

Case Study: The Corporate Spy

Khadia Usura is the director of a Fortune 500 company's main library and a renowned specialist in marketing research. He is often able to ferret out data and information that professional information brokers have missed. He uses every means at his disposal including serials, monographs, and reports, public and subscription data bases, governmental online sources (some of which are unavailable to the general public), international telephone and online contacts, a network of colleagues who help him so that he may in turn help them, and hired detectives who have their own contacts. Usura is obsessed with success, which in this case means that he must get all of the information that his clients, i.e., his superiors, have requested, even if the ways in which it is acquired are rather unsavory. Competitive intelligence is an accepted way of gathering information; it is not only perfectly legal, but some government agencies actually spy for American corporations, so Usura has no compunctions concerning his consultants who may use technology or flattery to wheedle information from competitors. It is legal but is it ethical?

---

sensitized to the subtleties of ethical decision making, and are not yet willing to spend $100,000 a year for a company ethicist. Thus, many business people are still willing to cut ethical corners; they may presume that their librarians are willing to do so too. They must not. They should adhere to the same principles that guide librarians generally. They might be expected to protect corporate secrets, but they must never entreat, unduly influence, bribe, extort, spy on, or otherwise attempt to elicit information from others. Librarians are, after all, not competitive intelligence agents or corporate spies. Even news media librarians may be asked to do objectionable research, ferret out information under false pretenses, violate confidentiality, or breach ethical tenets in other ways (Bornstein, 1999). The business community has a long way to go before it garners the complete respect of its customers. Corporate librarians can lead the way by refusing to capitulate to situational necessities.

Ethical Consistency

Law, medical, corporate, and other specialized collections appear to require a reorientation of some traditional ethical commitments on the part of information specialists. Closed collections, delimited or tiered reference service, refusals to help or recommend, and unequivocal protection of proprietary information may be warranted under certain exigent conditions, but all other mandates that order and control the information professions remain in force. Information access, quality of service, integrity of materials, protection of confidentiality and privacy, avoidance of conflicts of interest, informed consent, and other expectations are not altered or obviated by the special ethical situations discussed above. A singular, necessary reorientation is not a warrant to abrogate all laws, rules, regulations, and ethical mandates that control the profession. Acceptable ethical transvaluations should be considered anomalies and as such we should attempt to eliminate as many of them as possible by offering normal service in special settings, and protecting ourselves in public and academic facilities by hiring professionals who have some training in legal or medical librarianship, by making signed disclaimers available, and in all libraries by precisely insuring against information malpractice suits (despite the additional cost), since liability issues are perhaps the single most important determinant for delimiting service. *Information Liability and Negligence,* Stuart Hannabuss's (in press) forthcoming extensive overview, will be a good source of information for those who wish to restructure, reorient, and reaccommodate.

8

· · · · · · · · · · · · ·

Special and Archival
Collections

If norms and ethical considerations differ in corporate, legal, and medical libraries, then they are radically transvalued in special and particularly archival collections. Many of the ethical mandates that obtain in a public, school, or academic environment are not operative for these esoteric collections of unusual, specialized, valuable, holographic, rare, or unique materials. Instead, items are protected and kept behind closed or locked doors, often in temperature and humidity controlled areas; they are only accessible at specified times and only to legitimate users (which means that age, sex, appearance, and other entirely irrelevant or illegal factors may affect a decision to allow access and use); patrons may have to identify themselves, so that anonymity is sacrificed; there are many rules in force controlling what may be brought into a reading room, what one may do, how one must act, and so on (for example, pens may be disallowed or photocopying and photographing may be scrupulously controlled); the requested material may be delimited, proscribed, or entirely off-limits, sometimes for decades. Owners may have donated invaluable documents to an archive with the proviso that their usage must be limited to specific scholars or that the privacy of certain people must be protected. Naturally, all of these considerations alter the ways in which curators and archivists must deal with their patrons.

Special and archival collections have much in common with museums except that most of the materials in libraries are paper-based and secreted, whereas museum artifacts, ranging in size from minuscule meteorites to enormous frescoes and models of dinosaurs, are openly displayed, sometimes on a rotating basis. Interestingly, some archives resemble museums, since they collect everything relevant to their mission; thus, small and large artifacts may end up in a library environment too. Books and similar items are also displayed, but in order to do serious research, one must have access to the complete text, not just an arbitrarily chosen page.

Imagine the reaction of the rare books librarian at Amherst College, where a volume of Audubon's *Birds of America* is on permanent display, were a patron to request that the double-elephant folio be removed from its case so that he or she could peruse it. It is highly improbable that the curator would comply, especially since the pages of this enormous book are periodically turned. I am certain that the same fate would meet the casual visitor to the Morgan Library in New York, if he or she excitedly asked to touch, skim through, or read a book of hours, a Gutenberg Bible, or a Dickens fascicle. Indeed, one must have permission to even enter the working collection at the Morgan, which entails prior communication and serious scholarly purpose. If the librarian does not think that there is any real reason for entry, then access will be denied. One might attempt to differentiate between private institutions open to the public at the librarians' discretion and state owned entities that are ostensibly accessible to anyone, but this is a futile exercise. The New York state archivist will not open the doors to a group of hooligans who want to fondle the state constitution.

Special Collections

Special collections is a broad rubric that encompasses any material that is set aside in its own, generally protected, area. Rare, valuable, endangered, or fragile items as well as gifts and purchases that are maintained as a unit are housed here. For example, the various drafts of Robert Penn Warren's novels are arranged on shelves in the special collections section of the Beinecke Library at Yale. Naturally, patrons do not have access to these rooms. At the University of Pittsburgh, small press publications are stored in special collections. And thousands of rare volumes on the history of science are collected in one secure location at the University of Oklahoma. If an unauthorized person were to enter the area, an alarm would sound, and the police would arrive immediately. Some of these works are so highly regarded that when they are displayed in the special collections area, they are removed and stored in the vault over night, and then they may be replaced in the display cabinet the next day. This fulfills the curator's obligation to protect unique and thus irreplaceable items. These include not only manuscripts and holographs but also incunabula as well as signed first editions and copies of books that have been annotated by the author or some other influential person. Anna Kavan's copy of *Ice*, for example, contains many handwritten comments indicating dissatisfaction with the printed version of her novel. *Ice* and many other Kavan materials can be found in the restricted area at the University of Tulsa library.

Maintaining individual items and small or larger collections in this way protects both the physical material as well as the integrity of the collection. Having one thousand volumes on disparate aspects of the Holocaust scattered throughout the stacks of half a dozen branch libraries at a large research institution is very different from the very same books maintained on the shelves of a Holocaust center reading room. Here, serendipitous connections would be immediately recognizable to anyone who merely skimmed the books' spines, regardless of how they were arranged. Subject collections such as this also make the researcher's task much easier, even though these books usually do not circulate.

The rules to which users must accede in these special areas are sometimes disconcerting, annoying, or frustrating. Administrators of these areas prefer banker's hours: a working attorney who lives in Evanston, and who can only get to Chicago on Sundays to pursue research at a special location, will find it impossible to gain access. There is no reason that this tradition must be maintained. Academic libraries are often open from seven in the morning until midnight. Special collections' hours are limited merely because it is inconvenient and financially inefficient to remain open for extended periods of time. But ethical decisions should not be based on convenience. In order to gain admittance to many of these collections, one must indicate a specific need. Such discriminatory filtering chills the research process, since it may dissuade some potential users from requesting permission, and if a person were turned away, that might influence his or her future attitudes and activities.

As noted above, things have changed during the last 25 years. In the past, it was possible to retrieve original manuscripts, even when the person was not doing original research. A scholar and bibliophile told me that he once requested that the *Lindisfarne Gospels* be brought to his table, and moments later he was able to turn the pages of this incomparable work. Today, a superb facsimile would appear. Most people would not be able to tell the difference, since even foxing and wormholes are reproduced. But for the bibliophile, a facsimile is inadequate. It is as if one were to view a perfect reproduction of the *Guidoriccio da Fogliano* on display at the Metropolitan. Viewing this facsimile in New York is not the same as standing before the original painting in Siena. Nevertheless, it is necessary to protect unique and fragile materials. Light, handling, oils, dirt, scuffing, dropping, and other potential harms will curtail possibilities for future generations. Careless use will destroy books very quickly; when treated with respect, papyrus, parchment, and even paper can last for millennia.

Professionals who work in this area are governed by the "Standards for Ethical Conduct for Rare Book, Manuscript, and Special Collection Libraries and Librarians," an overly detailed, casuistic code that attempts to account for every ethical eventuality. Like the American Bar Association's dictates, it is much too controlling to allow responsible and accountable professionals to make tenable ethical decisions. And like the ethical requirements of the legal profession, which can change dramatically, so that advertising, which was once grounds for disbarment, is now an accepted practice, those mandates to which special collections professionals must adhere may alter. A casuistic code precludes necessary ethical adjustments.

Archives

Archives are similar to rare books and other special collections, except that much of their material is original, holographic, and unique. Sometimes, documents comprising hundreds or even thousands of linear feet remain unexamined, uncataloged, unindexed, or unavailable to users. Archives may automatically acquire or purchase individual items or collections, but frequently valuable papers and correspondence relating to an individual, an organization, or a corporation are donated, and along with the physical objects come lots of proscriptions. Donors may not want anyone to view their gifts until everyone mentioned is dead; thus they stipulate that 50 or 100 years must pass before the papers are opened to scholars or the public. Others, especially relatives, may not want unsympathetic readers to learn about their parents' or uncles' sexual affairs, their plagiaries, or their difficulties in composition. Perhaps a donor will stipulate that only a biographer whom he or she approves may read some diaries; and the final version of the biography may be subject to vetting. Even those who appear on the front pages of supermarket tabloids want to sanitize their eternal images.

If the archivist is to succeed in convincing a donor, whether it is the individual or his or her heir or executor, to contribute a collection, then

Case Study: Unreasonable Rules

As a graduate student, Lyngren Johnson discovered that no full-length biography had been written on Radwell Seron, a little-known but influential twentieth century man of letters. Now Johnson was an assistant professor at a large research institution and he was compelled to publish vast quantities of incomprehensible, post-modern gibberish. But he also wanted to make a real contribution to American literary history and so he contacted the prestigious institution where Seron's complete papers are housed. He received a courteous reply granting him permission to read the materials. The letter explained that more than eighty percent of the documents were indexed in finding lists, and the remainder were chronologically arranged in folders, and thus were easily accessible.

During his next long summer vacation, Johnson arrived in Boston, arranged for living accommodations, and proceeded to the university. He was greeted by the archivist, who explained the rules and requested that Johnson review, sign, and notarize the agreement. Johnson read through the single sheet and signed in front of the archivist, who is a notary. He then placed all of his belongings in a cabinet and went to the reading room door. The archivist was about to open it, when he turned and said, "Would you be kind enough to leave that pencil and paper in your pocket in the cabinet?" Johnson was nonplused: "But I will need them to take notes."

"Dr. Johnson, you just signed an agreement that stipulates that no miniature photocopiers, cameras, food, drink, or other materials are allowed in the reading room when accessing the Seron papers."

"I did not realize that that included a small pad and pencil. How will I record the details I cannot easily recall: foreign names, dates, and other minutiae that are crucial for a biographical account?"

The archivist scowled sympathetically: "I do not know. The donor stipulated that all of Seron's papers, even those personal letters that discuss embarrassing matters, are open to any legitimate scholar, but that nothing may be copied. When I explained that this would make research very difficult, she said she was not interested in scholarship. She wanted to make certain that nothing was ever stolen and by not allowing anything into the reading room, she thought that nothing would leave. I argued with her on at least three occasions, and then gave up.

I did not want to lose a valuable collection that includes holographic correspondence from Eliot, Auden, and Ginsberg. I am sorry."

the archivist must agree to these sometimes awkward, unrealistic, unfair, and unethical proscriptions. Collections may be sealed and unexamined until the temporal constraints are lifted, which means that current scholarship may be grossly distorted. On the other hand, if a conservative and demanding donor did not believe that his or her requirements would be fulfilled, it is quite possible that all of the documents would be destroyed. Although many authors sell, auction, or donate their papers before they die, others, who care less about money or posterity, burn them. Franz Kafka ordered Max Brod to destroy everything that he left behind, but after Kafka died, Brod could not bring himself to deprive readers of what turned out to be the most prescient and influential *oeuvre* of the twentieth century.

This general secretiveness is exaggerated by government bureaucrats who classify every document that flits across their desks. The Commission on Protecting and Reducing Government Secrecy has recommended delimiting classification to critical documents and declassifying innumerable items that would be useful to historical researchers (Martin, 1997). Interestingly, even non-classified governmental documents are sometimes difficult to access despite the good intentions of the Freedom of Information Act, which is often ignored, misinterpreted, or distorted by agency employees, who have too much discretion when it comes to real compliance.

The various delimitations operative in both special and archival collections stand in direct contrast to the theoretical and practical open access provided in most library environments. The reasons for these proscriptions are clear and defensible, and yet they may result in controlled usage, censored publications, and distorted scholarship. Since human beings are able to manipulate their psyches and excuse or rationalize almost anything, perhaps the current archival ethos should be reexamined. Strict control of historical documents in order to protect, for example, a previously sullied reputation, is really a misapplication of archival obligations. Ethical strictures should logically demand that material be made accessible to anyone who cares to use it. Modern practice has slowly eroded this obligation so that now archives protect and defend rather than offer open access to legitimate patrons.

Reference

Archivists, like general reference librarians, answer questions, provide guidance and advice, and may even connect researchers with each other. Since the ethos here is different than in a typical library setting, unusual ethical challenges may arise. In an incisive and replete essay, Elena Danielson (1997) discusses some of the problems that frequently appear in the literature, as well as other more esoteric cases. Like peer reviewers, who dismiss their colleagues' manuscripts because they infringe on the reviewers' own scholarship, archivists may disallow scholarly competitors from viewing specific materials; they may also vie with their employers for the same collections, if they run a business on the side, or collect.

All of these activities, naturally, constitute blatant conflicts of interest, and are unethical. Danielson observes that the size of our collections may preclude a comprehensive and complete search. Thus, it is not really possible to indicate to a patron that specific documents are <u>not</u> available, since they may be hidden away or lost in thousands of linear feet of similar reports, drafts, bills, papers, or correspondence. The quality and quantity of reference service is very different here; it depends on the patron, his or her needs, and the time available. And recommending specific materials may be analogous to offering medical or legal advice. Finally, mounting and maintaining an archival web page requires training and time. Once patrons can search though finding aids online, they may inundate the archives with reference queries that cannot be answered, because of lack of staff.

Privacy

Because archives collect materials that were not created for public consumption, the archivist may be ethically obligated to protect the privacy of the previous owners, heirs, participants in studies, as well as third parties— those who may appear in papers and correspondence in a negative light. In an excellent overview of privacy issues of publicly archived materials, Heather MacNeil (1992) observes that the general ethos has changed and now more private material is demanded and expected, for example, by social scientists; despite this, the laws governing archival privacy remain confusingly disparate, which creates difficult ethical situations for archivists whose predicated job is to make materials available but who are concomitantly governed by laws as well as a professional and human obligation to protect people from real harm. Anonymization and special limitations or agreements can help here. MacNeil suggests that archivists must be sensitive and respectful to the individuals documented, create guidelines, and allow a board to review confidentiality breaches on a case by case basis.

The Internet makes it possible for an archive to broadly disseminate its existence, catalogues, indexes, finding lists, and even the documents.

If a library decided to mount its collection of *Canterbury Tales* manuscripts along with some related scholarly papers from a group of Renaissance editors, no harm could follow. But if it chose to offer the personal papers of Sylvia Plath or Albert Einstein, some people might suffer psychological harm or embarrassment. Material that should be protected is often released. I once sent a critical letter to an official and a copy to the affected person. Someone mounted this confidential document on a publicly accessible web site, where it now resides.

Preservation

Preservation is a surprisingly complex topic. Here, we must deal with the environment in which materials are housed, the protection of the books, manuscripts, and papers from harm, theft, degradation, and destruction, and the means by which paper and digital materials are made accessible. Although these are extremely different topics, the goal is to protect artifacts so that they will be usable in the near and distant future. Insistence upon security measures against bad intentions is the first line of defense; otherwise, archivists are only ensuring that vandals and thieves will find materials in pristine condition. Those who control the destiny of documents react very differently to their charges. For example, in 1987, I requested a file of Carson McCullers's letters at the New York Public Library. The woman retrieved the folder, handed it to me, and turned away intending to leave.

I was nervous with these valuable materials, standing alone in a reading room from which I might easily have exited, and so I asked her to wait while I glanced through the typed and signed letters. Some years later, at the same institution but in a different collection, I wanted to ascertain the value of a Beckmann print. Here, the officious attendants hovered nearby observing me, which made me feel like a potential criminal. It is necessary to protect documents and media, but continuous observation or electronic surveillance creates an unhealthy atmosphere in which scholarly endeavors are stifled (Rude & Hauptman, 1993).

Preservation against the ravages of light, pests, human and natural disaster, and time is an ethical imperative, and curators and archivists have always taken these possibilities into account when administering their materials. During the last 50 years, increasing emphasis has been placed upon preservation techniques and it would be an inept specialist indeed who discounted preservation and the many new ways in which we are able to protect materials. These include environmental controls, acid-free storage containers, chemical treatments, copying, secondary storage, and so on. The advent of new media presents what appear to be insurmountable challenges, but to give up in the face of a hundred formats and series of outmoded reading devices is to capitulate to data loss, which is precisely what an archivist is committed to avoid. Audio and video tapes, electronic mail, journals, and documents, and more ephemeral and transitory texts such as interactive exchanges, as well as purposely altered items on hard drives or CD-ROMs, plus the soft- and hardware to read all of this, requires a substantial financial and intellectual commitment on the part of the private and public archivist.

Lamentably, it is probable that in a few hundred years, paper copies of various legal documents from the 18th, 19th, or 20th century will be available, but much that has only been electronically preserved will be inaccessible even if it still exists in digital form on some storage medium. That some early digital data is now unreadable because we no longer have the hardware to access it is a sound omen for future disaster. Deanna Marcum (1997) reminds us that the transitory nature of digital data additionally requires authentication and protection. This means that even an in-house system may require firewalls, black boxes, and passwords. Peter Mazikana (1997) offers some good advice for all electronic archives, but is especially prescient on Third World environments where computerization and electronic storage is still in its infancy.

The Library of Congress should be both the metaphorical and physical leader in the fight to preserve our historical, cultural, and intellectual heritage, and it certainly does play an active role both theoretically and practically. And yet, two shocking incidents indicate that there is room for improvement.

Theft and vandalism, as noted above, are two major sources of harm to our collections. Administrators are aware of this and when alerted that there are problems they must react immediately and proactively. In 1992, Deborah Maceda, a security officer at the Library of Congress, reported that she had noticed an increase in the number of vandalized books. Instead of rewarding Maceda and doing something about these crimes, she was reprimanded. Bear in mind that in 1995, some 300,000 books were missing from the LC collections (Gleick, 1995). More recently, a Congressional agency had to order the LC to make alterations in order to eliminate fire hazards that threaten extremely valuable materials, including a Gutenberg Bible and Jefferson's own collection, not to mention the lives of employees and patrons (Library, 2001). What these two incidents show is that acidity, pests, outmoded storage media, and antique hardware are not as crucial as we might superficially think. The first line of defense is

Code of Ethics for Archivists

THE SOCIETY OF
AMERICAN ARCHIVISTS

600 South Federal, Suite 504
Chicago, Illinois 60605
(312) 922-0140

*Adopted by
the Council of
the Society of
American Archivists,
1992*

Activists select, preserve, and make available documentary materials of long-term value that have lasting value to the organization or public that the archivist serves. Archivists perform their responsibilities in accordance with statutory authorization or institutional policy. They subscribe to a code of ethics based on sound archival principles and promote institutional and professional observance of these ethical and archival standards.

Archivists arrange transfers of records and acquire documentary materials of long-term value in accordance with their institutions' purposes, stated policies, and resources. They do not compete for acquisitions when competition would endanger the integrity or safety of documentary materials of long-term value, or solicit the records of an institution that has an established archives. They cooperate to ensure the preservation of materials in repositories where they will be adequately processed and effectively utilized.

Archivists negotiating with transferring officials or owners of documentary materials of long-term value seek fair decisions based on full consideration of authority to transfer, donate, or sell; financial arrangements and benefits; copyright; plans for processing; and conditions of access. Archivists discourage unreasonable restrictions on access or use, but may accept as a condition of acquisition clearly stated restrictions of limited duration and may occasionally suggest such restrictions to protect privacy. Archivists observe faithfully all agreements made at the time of transfer or acquisition. Archivists establish intellectual control over their holdings by describing them in finding aids

and guides to facilitate internal controls and access by users of the archives.

Archivists appraise documentary materials of long-term value with impartial judgment based on thorough knowledge of their institutions' administrative requirements or acquisitions policies. They maintain and protect the arrangement of documents and information transferred to their custody to protect its authenticity. Archivists protect the integrity of documentary materials of long-term value in their custody, guarding them against defacement, alteration, theft, and physical damage, and ensure that their evidentiary value is not impaired in the archival work of arrangement, description, preservation, and use. They cooperate with other archivists and law enforcement agencies in the apprehension and prosecution of thieves.

Archivists respect the privacy of individuals who created, or are the subject of, documentary materials of long-term value, especially those who had no voice in the disposition of the materials. They neither reveal nor profit from information gained through work with restricted holdings.

Archivists answer courteously and with a spirit of helpfulness all reasonable inquiries about their holdings, and encourage use of them to the greatest extent compatible with institutional policies preservation of holdings, legal considerations, individual rights, donor agreements, and judicious use of archival resources. They explain pertinent restrictions to potential users, and apply them equitably.

Archivists endeavor to inform users of parallel research by others using the same materials, and, if the individuals

concerned agree, supply each name to the other party.

As members of a community of scholars, archivists may engage in research, publication, and review of the writings of other scholars. If archivists use their institutions' holdings for personal research and publication, such practices should be approved by their employers and made known to others using the same holdings. Archivists who buy and sell manuscripts personally should not compete for acquisitions with their own repositories, should inform their employers of their collecting activities, and should preserve complete records of personal acquisitions and sales.

Archivists avoid irresponsible criticism of other archivists or institutions and address complaints about professional or ethical conduct to the individual or institution concerned, or to a professional archival organization.

Archivists share knowledge and experience with other archivists through professional associations and cooperative activities and assist the professional growth of others with less training or experience. They are obligated by professional ethics to keep informed about standards of good practice and to follow the highest level possible in the administration of their institutions and collections. They have a professional responsibility to recognize the need for cooperative efforts and support the development and dissemination of professional standards and practices.

Archivists work for the best interests of their institutions and their profession and endeavor to reconcile any conflicts by encouraging adherence to archival standards and ethics.

precisely the same as it was in the Alexandrian Library: We must protect against human intervention and physical disaster.

Code of Ethics for Archivists

Archivists have their own concise code, which offers guidance on their highly specialized professional obligations. Among other points, it discusses the acquisitions of collections, open and restricted access, appraisal, security, privacy, and conflicts of interest. As is usual in most professions, there is no means of enforcement should a member of the Society of American Archivists refuse to abide by its code's various exhortations. Additionally, I doubt whether membership in the SAA is a prerequisite for archival employment.

9

Research and Publication

Practitioners and theoreticians of librarianship are interested in improving and honoring the profession. This is accomplished in an academic environment is by providing a foundational basis for the worthiness of the discipline. Librarianship rests on a solid grounding of pragmatic and empirical conclusions that have been reduced to some viable foundational constructs. But even our profession's most avid defenders would be forced to admit that it is neither nuclear engineering nor molecular biology.

Theory is confirmed in empirical experimentation at the particle accelerator or in the genetics laboratory and these results become the basis for applications. In librarianship, theory only carries us so far and empirical verification is often superfluous. It is possible to function quite well without either of these attributes; we can fulfill our tasks without empirical studies and foundational documents, for, lamentably, the major changes that have occurred in the dissemination, storage, and retrieval of data and information have come about because information and computer scientists have made astonishing progress in technical theory and applications, many of which have subsequently been implemented by commercial concerns interested in reaping extraordinary profits.

For almost two hundred years, scholars and even laypersons have showered the hard sciences with unequivocal respect. First, astronomy, physics, and chemistry, and later geology and biology were placed at the top of an imaginary scholarly hierarchy. The scientific method reaped wonders in these arenas, and so those who studied human behavior decided that they would import what at times is an entirely inappropriate modality in order to study people and their interactions. Social scientists such as anthropologists, sociologists, and psychologists as well as economists, political scientists, and even historians usurp the scientist's arsenal, reduce people to measurable entities, and draw unwarranted conclusions about human beings generally. Library scientists saw an opening and jumped on board the empirical bandwagon. Research and publication legitimize the profession. And so we have hundreds of magazines and journals filled with articles, essays, investigations, reports, surveys, overviews, and critiques of other articles and monographs—a replete armamentarium to rival almost any discipline. We also believe that research and publication should be rewarded and so in an academic environment, those who write and publish are tenured and promoted. Those who do not, find other work.

In 1942, Robert Merton (1973) published a groundbreaking essay in which he observed that scientists adhere to a group of positive norms such as communal sharing and disinterested research. Many years later, Ian Mitroff (1974) proved that this analysis is wishful thinking; subsequently, even pure scientists like Pasteur, who refused to profit from his discoveries, have been shown to deviate from the ideal norms postulated by Merton. The problem with scientists is that they are human and prone to all of the seductions to which any person might succumb. Honor, awards, power, and financial gain may entrap almost anyone, and the demands for reward have increased dramatically during the past half century. Scientific research is tedious and plodding, and only occasionally does one make a truly great discovery.

One of the ways to speed up the process is to embellish. For decades, scientists vehemently insisted that virtually no one was guilty of misconduct. The argument is that among millions of researchers, only a minuscule percentage ever do anything dishonest. Even if this were true, at a time when we publish millions of papers each year, a tiny percentage is still a lot of misinformation. And if only one or two of those papers influence a discipline to, for example, medicate the retarded, when that is precisely what we should not do, then a great deal of harm has resulted from just a few distortions. But as it happens, the small percentage is much larger than scientists were willing to admit. A broad array of these respected people, especially those in biomedicine, are guilty of sloppy record keeping, data manipulation (fudging, trimming, cooking), fabrication, plagiarism, dissimulation, and theft. The social scientists who misappropriate the scientific method are also prone to these aberrant behaviors, and so anthropologists, for example, have been accused of allowing their ethnographic subjects to deceive them (Freeman, 1999) and harming indigenous peoples (Tierney, 2000). Researchers in librarianship are social scientists; they too may be seduced into misconduct.

Librarianship and the Search for Knowledge

The most fervent proponent of the application of the scientific method in the pursuit of empirically derived data in librarianship is Peter Hernon, who edits, among other publications, *The Journal of Academic Librarianship* and *Library and Information Science Research*. Given the foregoing discussion and Hernon's advocacy, one would suspect that he would vehemently deny the possibility that researchers in our profession are capable of misconduct. But as it happens, Hernon is the first scholar to seriously question researcher integrity in librarianship. He is also interested in the effect that general research misconduct has on our collections.

In a groundbreaking essay, written with Ellen Altman (Hernon & Altman, 1995), and subsequently in *Research Misconduct: Issues, Implications, and Strategies* (Altman & Hernon, 1997), he investigates, analyzes, and discusses a variety of germane possibilities in order to discover or forestall. This prescient attitude is praiseworthy and can serve as a paradigm for other disciplines where ethical consideration lags far behind methodological or technological sophistication. For example, anthropology, sociology, psychology, history, physics and chemistry, and literary studies are all ripe for the nurturing and growth of research misconduct. In none of these disciplines is this probability given the respect that it deserves, and there are no real, viable means in place to ferret out and punish miscreants. Indeed, in many cases the powerful professional

---

How to Avoid Research Misconduct

1. Check and recheck procedures and data meticulously.
2. Do not fudge, cook, or trim data.
3. Do not fabricate.
4. Do not plagiarize.
5. Do not abuse the privilege of peer review.
6. Do not republish.
7. Respect the conventions of the discipline, journal, and publisher.
8. Document sources correctly and meticulously.
9. Respect the needs of editors and authors.

organizations refuse to condemn perpetrators in any meaningful way for fear of legal actions that would bankrupt them. Enforcement of rules, regulations, and codes is nonexistent. Involved scholars will argue that very few ethical breaches turn up in astrophysics or Scandinavian studies, and they may be correct. But given the trend in biomedicine and literary work, the ease with which one can plagiarize, and the fact that an extremely high percentage of American students is believed to cheat in some way, it would be surprising indeed if researchers did not occasionally accommodate themselves to a very profitable situation.

Scholars in library and information science are either educators or practitioners. The former are compelled to make discoveries and publish their results so that they can achieve tenure and promotions, but this is also true of tenure track practitioners, and even librarians who do not have faculty status may be forced to publish. Finally, there are many professionals who have something to say regardless of their work environment. In order to succeed with the most prestigious journals, one must adhere to the traditional research paradigm, which is inculcated in master's and especially doctoral programs. Even those pursuing historical or qualitative modalities must not veer too far from the conservative line. So we set up pseudo-scientific experiments or survey some willing participants, we randomize, control, double blind, and use lots of impressive terminology; we ascertain, apply statistical measures, analyze, and, finally, draw conclusions. A few hundred diverse library users fill out a form or speak briefly with an interviewer and we generalize that all patrons prefer OPACS, feel uncomfortable in the presence of pornography, or would rather do their research at home. Sometimes the inductions are valid and useful, but since human beings are not ball bearings or electrons, their behavior and their articulated beliefs are neither predictable nor necessarily reliable, despite appearances. Sometimes even animals act perversely just to mess up an experiment.

Educators and scholars in library and information studies model their research on the social science paradigm and attempt to adhere as closely as possible to the stringent requirements inherited from the hard sciences, generally, even when doing qualitative studies. We have believed that scientific research will save us. The problem is that the paradigm has changed: we now recognize that traditional scientific norms are unrealistic, objectivity is an impossibility, and librarianship is not a neutral discipline (Dick, 1995). Additionally, feminists have called for a reorientation in methodology: "Essentially, the library profession needs to devise a clearer and better concept of how we conduct research...." (Hannigan & Crew, 1993, p. 28). Revising the ways in which we pursue our scholarly work will help us to avoid wasting time on irrelevancies, misusing and abusing other disciplines' methods and tools (Sandstrom & Sandstrom, 1995), and deceiving ourselves that what we are doing has real applicability. It is unnecessary and unethical to investigate, record, analyze, structure, conclude, write, and disseminate material for its own sake or merely to achieve tenure and promotion.

When the unreasonable demand to publish creates unbearable pressure on young academics, they may attempt to solve the problem by falsifying, fabricating, or plagiarizing. When queried, a high percentage of academics indicate that they know of someone who is guilty of some form of research misconduct. Hernon and his co-editor, Candy Schwartz, interviewed seven board members of *Library and Information Science Research* (Burke et al., 1996). Surprisingly, not one of the interviewees knew of a case of misconduct in our field nor did they think that it is a real problem, although some fudging and inadequate work does occur. And yet, they admitted that detecting such flagrant transgressions during the refereeing process is extremely difficult. The logical conclusion, then, might be that there is some misconduct in our profession; we just have not discovered it yet.

There are two aspects of research misconduct that do not overly concern disciplinary scholars but which are of dramatic importance to information professionals. First, as the guardians of knowledge, we probably

---

Case Study: My Tenure Depends upon Your Speedy Decision

Laura Tipo is in her fifth year at an excellent college where librarians have faculty status; they therefore must fulfill all of the normal requirements for tenure and promotion. During her time here, two colleagues acted as mentors, offering good advice and suggestions. They tried to induce Tipo to do the requisite research and writing that would lead to publication, but with the exception of three brief and inconsequential papers, she spent all of her time on other matters. Soon her dean and the academic vice-president were to decide whether to grant tenure, so Tipo finally reworked her excellent master's thesis and submitted it to one of the most prestigious library science publications. She waited. After two months, she anxiously called the editor, who courteously explained that the review process could take up to six months with an additional period required for a tentative decision and rewriting if necessary. Even then, there was no guarantee of publication. Tipo explained that her career depended on the editor's decision, and she asked him if he could speed up the process. He silently wondered what she had been doing during the previous five years.

should be doing something about contamination, but are enjoined by the ethical strictures imposed upon us by the ALA. Hernon and Altman (1999) are concerned that many discredited studies continue to infect the literature and therefore the collections; if librarians do not alert patrons that an article is flawed or retracted, who will? And second, these same scholars insist that misconduct perpetrated by scholars in all disciplines has an adverse effect on the quality of service that librarians render, since the collections and reference personnel are disseminating disinformation (Hernon & Altman, 1995). The authors list 59 sources that have published material by scholars guilty of misconduct; with few exceptions, all of these are biomedical publications and include *Science, Nature, The Lancet, Cell,* and others of similar stature.

There are big rewards in store for those who publish in the right journals, build upon their reputations, and continue to turn out influential work. The seductions that misconduct offers are evident in other fields. Librarianship may be in the process of building a body of knowledge based on misperception, faulty methodology, error, statistical distortion, and purposeful misconduct. If this is not the case yet, then it is impossible to deny that the general ethos in which we operate may soon lead down the easy road that an astonishing number of scholars in other disciplines have chosen to follow. Peter Hernon and Ellen Altman have alerted us to this very real possibility. By sensitizing students, educators, and practitioners to the mores of the profession and the necessity that truth is the scholars' goal, we may be able to avoid the disasters that have recently embarrassed other professions.

Authors

Misconduct would be less enticing if publication for tenure and promotion purposes was deemphasized; then only those who had something to say or authors with a creative drive would feel compelled to write and disseminate their discoveries or ideas. Another possibility is for departments, institutions, organizations, funding agencies, the federal government, journal editors and publishing houses to take a much harder line. For example, if someone were found guilty of submitting a plagiarized paper to a library science publication, this fact would be made available to other editors, all of whom would refuse to accept material from the plagiarist. Federal law could mandate stricter punishments rather than the slap on the hand now meted out to the dishonest National Institutes of Health grant recipient.

Realistically, neither of these solutions is likely to occur in the near future, and so it is up to individual authors to avoid misconduct in order to ensure the integrity of the literature and to protect themselves from potential harm. The pedagogical system, from the earliest grades through postdoctoral work, should emphasize ethical commitment, honesty, integrity, and precise documentation procedures, and deemphasize experimental success, publication, grants, and awards. Scholarly values should be inculcated and the fear of retribution (failure, expulsion) should help to control the wayward. When students become scholars, they will remember the general message offered over the course of the preceding 20 years. And if ethical commitment should prove lacking, stringent legal sanctions can be extremely convincing.

Scholars must be scrupulously careful as they observe, analyze, and record data; sloppy record keeping is tantamount to misconduct, since the negative consequences may be equally damaging. Authors should avoid the easy seductions that allow for the manipulation of data through blatant creation when experimental results are unavailable or various alterations to statistics at the .01 or .001 place. Rounding is an acceptable procedure, but it should be consistent and not an excuse to purposely manipulate data in favor of the hypothesis. Plagiary is anathema: Scholars should never inadvertently or purposely pick up the ideas or words of another person and attempt to pass them off as their own. The excuse cited most often in these bizarre and convoluted cases is that the author must have recorded something from a source, failed to note the ascription, and then months or years later incorporated the statements into the article or monograph innocently believing that this was a brilliant insight he or she had long ago. Meticulous documentation at every stage of the research and writing process is obviously the first line of defense for those who really care about the niceties of acknowledgement.

Editors

Most editors begin their careers as authors, and so they are intimately acquainted with the problems and tensions involved with querying, submitting manuscripts, reading reviewers' comments and suggestions, revising, and awaiting publication. Not surprisingly, though, once they take command of a journal, they forget the traumas that authors must endure, and commence to heap abuse upon the very people who make their publication possible. They ignore contributors and their pleas, promise more then they can deliver, respond belatedly or rudely, make unreasonable demands, steal ideas, and generally treat authors with little or no consideration. This general attitude is so common that when an editor acts precisely as editors ought to act, it astonishes. Editors have good reason to disrespect authors, since the latter are often extremely unreliable; by the time one is a mature scholar, he or she ought to write mellifluously, spell correctly, document completely, avoid plagiary, and enclose a legible copy of the manuscript along with a disk or whatever else the journal requires. But these sophisticated academics and freelancers often fail to accommodate themselves to the editors' requirements, which results in annoyance and cynicism. These two negative attitudes reinforce each other and the vicious cycle is very difficult to break.

Editors should make an effort to treat contributors fairly, judiciously, and competently. Failing to render a decision after eight or ten months has elapsed, even if a reviewer refuses to respond, is unethical. The scholarship is aging and the author is worrying about tenure, promotion, and other career necessities. Continually promising to complete the process but failing to do so while allowing the blame to devolve upon others is an extreme abuse of the power vested in the editor by the sponsoring institution, the publisher, or his or her peers. If organizational skills are wanting, if physical, psychological, or temporal demands limit an editor's ability to function efficiently, he or she should find some other vocation.

Peer Reviewers

Referees offer their services to journals, monograph publishers, and granting agencies in order to assure the quality and integrity of the discipline and its literature. Infrequently, referees are remunerated, but generally they tirelessly scrutinize and comment on manuscripts with few tangible rewards. From a cynically pragmatic point of view, reviewers would be much better off doing research or writing another paper of their own, since academic evaluation cares very little for refereeing; what counts here is publication, both because it is inherently praiseworthy and because some publication brings with it direct monetary rewards from stipends, honoraria, advances, and royalty payments. Because peer reviewers get little for their effort, they often fail to come through. They lose manuscripts, do not return their remarks in a timely fashion, render dishonest decisions to protect colleagues or their own scholarship, and steal ideas. Nevertheless, editors cannot shift the blame to referees when the process breaks down; these people perform a philanthropic service for editors who sometimes earn substantial salaries, subsidies, or release time. If a referee proves to be unreliable, the editor should immediately locate another, one who will return manuscripts along with useful comments within a few weeks. If a scholar cannot live up to stringent demands, he or she should not volunteer to act as a peer reviewer. Publish or perish is not just a witty apothegm. Peer review is in trouble, because it does not work well: it delays publication, inhibits iconoclastic ideas, fails to control quality, ignores misconduct, and is replete with ethical misdeeds; all of this is recognized by the American Medical Association, which recently held three conferences on the topic.

Documentation

Most critics and commentators who take an interest in epistemic integrity would be unequivocal in their condemnation of carelessness, sloppiness, inefficiency, and inadvertent mistakes, errors, or omissions that result in flawed conclusions as well as a host of purposeful deceptions, all of which constitute research misconduct. But many of these same scholars would be more forgiving when it comes to inept documentation. This is rather surprising given the fact that error and misconduct are ignored in most disciplines,* whereas documentation is stressed even in some high school writing classes. Acknowledging sources and attributing direct quotations or ideas has been a requirement in Western scholarship since the Renaissance. Even during the medieval period, scribes and readers would annotate manuscripts with glosses and historians and theologians would attribute ideas to earlier thinkers such as Herodotus or Aquinas, either because they did not wish to deceive or because these references buttressed their arguments. In traditional Biblical exegesis, citing Rashi or the Rambam is an easy way to convince a reader or listener that the articulated perspective is on target. Virtually all humanists, social scientists, and scientists agree that documenting sources plays a crucial role in scholarly communication.

There are more than 200 different systems used to indicate to a reader that the material derives from another source. Some of these are very dissimilar and others resemble each other so closely that an outsider might wonder why it was necessary to make such minor alterations. The humanities uses the Modern Language Association (MLA) style, which is based, in part, on the American Psychological Association (APA) format. Both of these have eliminated footnotes and require in-text documentation to lead the reader to the correct references noted at the conclusion of the work. Psychologists adhere scrupulously to APA style, whereas sociologists have a slightly different format. Psychologists, by the way, probably

---

*During 15 years of college and graduate work in a diversity of disciplines in three different countries, I only encountered error analysis in physics and misconduct in a sociology of science class.

do the best job of creating citations in conformance with their mandated style. A diversity of biology periodicals require their own individual variations on another slightly different system. Some monograph publishers require authors to conform to Chicago style, and journalists use the AP format.

With so many conflicting systems, it is hardly surprising that problems occur. Undergraduates are either taught or requested to use a particular method and they are successful to a greater or lesser extent. Once the class is over, the system goes into hibernation; if it is never required again, eventually it is lost. Graduate students ostensibly master the format that they must apply in their theses or dissertations and one might reasonably expect that this knowledge would stay with them, especially if they remain academics and teach their own students how to document correctly and criticize the technical errors that may appear in the students' bibliographies. Thus, it is extremely difficult to explain the anomalies, perversions, and teratisms that riddle the references found in manuscripts submitted by scholars, or the omissions, distortions, and outright errors that appear even in the published versions, which may have gone through a rigorous peer review. Bizarre alterations in the discipline's system are annoying and even offensive, but careless errors in names, titles, volume numbers, dates, and pagination are an indication that the author is not fully committed to the work he or she is doing. These errors confuse and harm the discipline's literature and contaminate its knowledge base.

Although some scholars are interested in the history of documentation (e.g., Grafton, 1997), very few seem to care about documentation integrity. Janell Rudolph and Deborah Brackstone (1990) are exceptions; they insist that they encounter incorrect citations, which makes it difficult or impossible to locate material, with great frequency. Their personal experiences are confirmed, they say, by studies that show "that bibliographic inaccuracy is extensive in scholarly articles" (p. A56). The error rate runs from 24 to 44.9 percent. Authors often miscite their own work and even the citation indexes may lead to dead ends.

Rudolph and Brackstone offer three useful suggestions: instructors should inculcate excellent bibliographic habits in students; authors should verify citations in their own work; and we should develop a universal system of documentation for all disciplines. Beverley Geer (1995) comes to much the same conclusions concerning lack of standardization, incorrect citations, and invalid research. Documentation makes it possible to trace the sources an author has used, and incorrect or invalid citations increase the difficulty of successfully locating material. In order to eliminate these problems, we are adjured to carefully verify whatever it is we are recording. In 1996, Richard Hamilton published a volume in which he traced the citations listed in Max Weber's *Protestant Ethic and the Spirit of Capitalism*, one of the seminal studies of the 20th century; he discovered that they did not lead to what might have been expected nor confirm the points Weber was making. Citations are the life blood of scholarship. Keep them crisp, accurate, and on target.

Conclusion

There can be no doubt that research and publication legitimize the profession, expand our knowledge base, and improve the services that we provide. But we may be overdoing things: We write and publish at a truly prodigious rate. Consider that Haworth Press, a small house that specializes, in part, in library and information science materials, offers some 400 journals to subscribers. Haworth is but one of a host of publishers catering to our field. Some of them produce thousands of reference books and monographs every year. Only a few of Elsevier's journals are germane to librarianship, but because this publisher appears to overcharge libraries, many information professionals would like to alter market conditions in order to lower prices. Very few authors, however, are willing to take a personal stand by refusing to publish in periodicals owned by companies such as Elsevier. Susan Martin is an exception. In a May 1999 *Journal of Academic Librarianship* (*JAL*) column, she informs readers that she and some of her colleagues will, on principle, henceforth disassociate themselves from *JAL*, which Elsevier has acquired. This is ethically commendable, but pragmatically useless: There is always someone more than willing to become a columnist for *JAL*, which is, after all, the premier general periodical aimed at academic librarians. If we had the courage of Martin's convictions, we would solve our serials crisis by canceling all overpriced journals en masse, and as scholars we would refuse to offer our manuscripts to publishers whom we believe are acting unethically.

10

Intellectual Property and Copyright

> Copyright [is] a legal concept that is intended to encourage the dissemination of information [but it may be] used instead as an instrument of censorship.
>
> — Robert W. Kastenmeier

In the Western world, creators and producers of physical or intellectual artifacts hold property rights in their work. If someone wishes to purchase, lease, or mass produce a better toaster oven then he or she must reimburse the person responsible for the new design. There are, naturally, many complications here, not the least of which is patent status, but the general idea is fair, ethical, and legally warranted: one ought to be remunerated for one's contributions. In this context, intellectual materials are legally different from physical entities, but the idea is the same: the person who articulates something of value ought to be compensated for its use. Thus, Hemingway's letters to Maxwell Perkins, his literary editor, may now belong physically to Perkins's heirs, but the articulations are the property of the Hemingway estate. The Perkins people may not publish or profit from the locutions without permission from the Hemingways. They may, however, sell or even barbarically destroy the artifacts themselves.

The framers of the Constitution realized that progress derives from discovery, invention, articulation, and publication. And some of them were undoubtedly aware of the history of the Stationers' Company as well as the Statute of Queen Anne in England (Bielefield & Cheeseman, 1993) and the *droit moral* in France. Thus, despite the extraordinary concision of the Constitution, they included a section on copyright. Constitutional law has been elucidated, amended, and expanded through statutory and case law so that copyright protection is now replete, complex, and ambiguous. Lamentably, instead of protecting the author or his or her heirs, it may offer unwarranted protection to large conglomerates that sometimes abuse and harm their freelance contributors, and then cite copyright as an excuse for limiting the legitimate use and application of their popular and scholarly publications.

The law impinges upon many library and archival functions, but nowhere is it more salient than in copyright issues. Although much that follows is tangentially concerned with legal matters, this discussion is intended to clarify the *ethical* mandates that should control library usage of ostensibly protected material. The law is a useful guide and should be followed despite its harsh demeanor, but it must never be confused with ethical commitment. If the federal statute mandates that it is illegal to copy a 600 page chemistry text (which one may be tempted to do because it is oppressively overpriced or because the publisher refuses to respond or because it is out of print), then, naturally, individuals, instructors, or librarians acting as representatives of their institutions are breaking the law and are therefore legally culpable, if they copy it. This does not mean that they are necessarily acting unethically, for the law and ethics are sometimes antipodal opponents. Countless examples of the ironic clash that exists between legal necessity and ethical commitment come to mind. It is, for example, against the law to purchase heroin because it is harmful and addictive, but American companies market tobacco products to adults in America and adolescents in Third World countries. It may be illegal to sell tobacco to teenagers, but American youngsters smoke and chew at an astonishing rate. Many of them become hooked for life on a harmful and addictive product. Or consider the Nazi era laws that mandated that German, Dutch, French, and other countries' citizens must turn in Jews, homosexuals, Roma, and the disabled so that they might be used as slave laborers or shipped to extermination camps. Lots of ostensibly good people adhered to the law because they were taught to do so or because they were afraid of acting contrarily or because they disliked these minority populations. On the other hand, some truly good people refused to capitulate to the barbaric mandates of the Third Reich and risked their own lives to help and hide the hunted. Civilians who adhered to the egregiously evil law did the wrong thing; those who defied the law acted ethically.

There are three points to bear in mind when considering libraries, copyright, and its infringement. First, an ethical commitment to the dissemination of information, an injunction that John Swan trumpeted as our profession's highest principle (Wiener, 1987), and against which I have often railed if and when it comes into conflict with more pressing social necessities, may require an apparent violation of the law, at least as it is interpreted by corporate attorneys and marketing specialists. Second, the contravention of the law is a dangerous business; it can lead an individual and his or her institution into costly civil or unpleasant criminal imbroglios. Third, a refusal to act ethically out of fear is a temporary refuge of the pusillanimous, and has no place in the life of a professional information specialist. The reader should not misconstrue the foregoing remarks. The purpose here is neither to subvert the law nor to suborn others into breaking it. But the law is ambiguous, fair use is open to broad interpretation, and users have rights that render the fair use doctrine otiose. We must take advantage of these anomalies in order to help patrons gain access to whatever it is they require.

Information may want to be free, but it is not. Someone works to create it and this costs money. Nevertheless, conservative interpretation of or slavish adherence to strictly legal mandates will inhibit our ethical commitment to disseminate information. We tread an ambiguous line because we pay for information and then are told by commercial vendors (who may not even hold individual copyright but rather simply indicate their demands in licensing agreements) that we may not distribute data, information, articles, or books in specific ways. The law may abet this travesty because copyright law has evolved through legislation forwarded by politicians who succumb either to their own agendas or to lobbyists who wish to protect the interests of their employers. This is a cynical attitude, but the legislative process is highly politicized and the results are always suspect, especially since unexamined or generally unacceptable addenda are hooked on to bills and manage to become law despite the fact that most of those voting affirmatively are against the ancillary portion of the new legislation.

Publishers offer some periodical subscriptions to individuals at fair and reasonable rates. Through differential pricing schemes, these same periodicals are sold to libraries and other institutions at double, triple, quadruple, or even ten times as much, so that a $50 quarterly can cost a collection $500 per year. The etiology for this is clear: many academic institutions require the material, have adequate funds to purchase what they need to support programs and pass accreditation evaluations, and so despite the high prices enough collections will subscribe to allow for a profit. But the implicit reasoning behind this is equally evident: individuals might share a journal with a colleague or student, but generally the individual subscriber will be the only reader; he or she will certainly not present it to a collection, because publishers have manipulated us into believing that this is unethical. They often protect themselves against this hazard by having individual subscribers sign statements to this effect in order to be eligible for the lower rate. This is perhaps the only case in general commerce where one must make a promise in order to purchase a product, a promise that is legally questionable. (This is reminiscent of the software inserts that insist that by opening the shrink-wrap packaging, the purchaser agrees to whatever the producer mandates. In both cases, consumers have only themselves to blame for allowing producers to get away with these schemes.) Precisely the opposite situation obtains in the institutional setting: no publisher ever sold a serial subscription to a library, laboratory, or special collection under the misguided belief that only one person would use it. Hundreds, thousands, even tens of thousands of people may consult a given reference tool or periodical issue during its lifetime, a period that may, in some cases, last hundreds of years. It is worth noting here that publishers do not especially like libraries since one purchase or subscription serves countless potential buyers or subscribers. But concomitantly, only libraries would tolerate or could afford the exorbitant costs currently charged for scientific journals. Thus, publishers, reasonably and logically, expect multiple readings of publications sold to collections. These brief remarks should be borne in mind when reading much that follows.

Copyright Law

The Constitution provides for copyright protection:

To promote the progress of science and the useful arts, by securing for limited time to authors and inventors the exclusive right to their respective writings and discoveries.

It is obvious from the wording that the primary purpose of this provision is not to offer protection to authors, but rather to ensure that intellectual progress is stimulated. The many subsequent legislative interpretations attempted to clarify and expand the protective aspect. The 1790 law is clear and helpful; the 1976 legislation is overly restrictive: it so scared administrators and scholars that shortly after its implementation, and in accordance with the law, warning signs were posted on library copiers, and professors questioned procedures they had followed for years. Although almost a quarter of a century has passed since F. Wilfrid Lancaster requested permission to distribute my infamous bomb experiment (Hauptman, 1976) to his class, his brief letter and my positive reply are as clear to me as if the incident had occurred this morning.

All of this concern was unwarranted, since the fair use doctrine incorporated into the 1976 law provides for reasonable usage of all kinds, including reprinting, republication, and copying by anyone who requires the material. This is especially the case for pedagogical purposes, but fair use is not limited exclusively to educators and students. People generally and even commercial concerns may reprint brief portions of a copyright holder's work. But as L. Ray Patterson and Stanley Lindberg (1991) point out:

> Corporate copyright owners and others with vested interests—including licensing agents, broadcasting and publishing associations, and so on—have used the skeletal statute, section 107 of the 1976 Copyright Act, to influence and promulgate guidelines that purport to implement that law but instead often constitute self-aggrandizement at the expense of the public interest [10].

They go on to explain that the "baselessly exaggerated copyright notices" (10) that corporations affix to their products tend to inhibit legal reproduction. But "users have rights that are just as important as those of authors and publishers—and these rights are grounded in the law of copyright" (11). Insisting that this is so or that corporations misconstrue, indeed pervert, the original intent of American copyright law does not give people the right to lift, plagiarize, steal, or kidnap intellectual property that does not belong to them. Using Napster and similar software in order to record CDs is theft.

In 1998, Congress passed the Digital Millennium Copyright Act, which further restricts a patron's ability to legitimately (ethically) use, in various ways, the material to which collections subscribe or which they lease or have purchased. In March 2001, a Virginia Congressman indicated that he would "introduce legislation" to counter this infringement of fair use (Flagg, 2001). Shortly thereafter, the Senate approved a bill that would allow educational institutions to delimit copyright restrictions on digital music and video (Foster, 2001, June 1).

Fair Use

The fair use doctrine, included in the 1976 copyright law, is applicable to commercial publication and usage. It is often noted, referred to, and cited when dealing with personal endeavors, but it is not relevant or necessary. Personal, non-commercial usage supercedes fair use (see below). Fair use permits commercial entities to include direct quotations, paraphrases, parodies, critiques, and commentaries in publications that they sell for profit. Nevertheless, Stephen Elias (1999), a lawyer, can insist that,

> Some uses of a copyrighted work are considered fair use — that is, the use is not legally considered to be an infringement because of its non-commercial or incidental nature. For example, fair use is often legitimate when a work is being used for teaching, research, scholarship, criticism or journalism [75].

This is extremely misleading, since the implication is that fair use applies only to non-commercial instances such as teaching and scholarship, and somehow journalism is either a philanthropic enterprise or has been hooked on to the other possibilities as a public service; or the usage is incidental, i.e., trivial. In truth, directly quoting or paraphrasing a portion of a book or article in a review, critical commentary, or exegesis is invariably a commercial venture since the new work is sold, and in the case of reviews, the avowed purpose is to induce readers to purchase the volume being discussed. The cited material is not only not incidental (except in length as proscribed by law), but instead, crucial to the discussion or argument, otherwise it could be eliminated. William Patry (1985) refutes Elias's position thus:

> The court of appeals did, however, make a particularly valuable point: A use whose 'character' is commercial may nevertheless have a 'purpose' of a type qualifying for fair use, e.g., criticism or comment. Under these circumstances, a proper 'purpose' may rebut an otherwise unacceptable commercial 'character' [367].

And generally speaking, authors of original works are elated to have reviewers and critics quote, paraphrase, and comment on their copyrighted publications, since these fair usages legitimize, popularize, and sell their creations.

Elias continues, "It's important to understand that fair use is a defense rather than an affirmative right" (75). This too is misleading. Fair use is not a proscriptive doctrine that controls what users may do; instead it is precisely the antithesis, providing as it does a limitation on the exclusive rights held in the copyrighted work; thus, it functions as a stimulus to the Constitutional mandate to promote science and the useful arts. If a patron requires a personal copy, there is no need to analyze his or her needs in

---

Copyright Law of 1976: Fair Use

§107. Limitations on exclusive rights: Fair use

Notwithstanding the provisions of section 106 and 106A, the fair use of a copyrighted work, including such use by reproduction in copies or phonorecords or by any other means specified by that section, for purposes such as criticism, comment, news reporting, teaching (including multiple copies for classroom use), scholarship, or research, is not an infringement of copyright. In determining whether the use made of a work in any particular case is a fair use the factors to be considered shall include—

(1) the purpose and character of the use, including whether such use is of a commercial nature or is for nonprofit educational purposes;
(2) the nature of the copyrighted work;
(3) the amount and substantiality of the portion used in relation to the copyrighted work as a whole; and
(4) the effect of the use upon the potential market for or value of the copyrighted work.

The fact that a work is unpublished shall not itself bar a finding of fair use if such finding is made upon consideration of all the above factors.

---

terms of this doctrine; if an instructor requires multiple copies for classroom distribution or to place on reserve, then he or library personnel should apply the four factors listed in the law (see sidebar, Copyright Law of 1976: Fair Use). It is obvious from the examples cited — phonorecords, criticism, news reporting — that one may reprint or reproduce copyrighted material for profit without infringing upon the law. Since this is the case and since the first of the four factors to consider when making a decision differentiates commercial from educational purposes — thereby validating pedagogical pursuits — the utilization of copyrighted material in an educational setting is unequivocally sanctioned. The three remaining factors are open to interpretation, since no specific guidelines are offered.

Photocopying

Individuals may copy a text in order to avoid purchasing it, but in most cases this is counterproductive. Reproducing a lengthy document can be more expensive than buying it, and it will be shoddy and unbound. (A person once naively informed me that since my *Ethical Challenges in*

Librarianship [Hauptman, 1988] was out of print, she simply photocopied the entire book.) But this, I believe, occurs infrequently. An extremely high percentage of copying from published sources is based entirely on our current infatuation with convenience. In the recent past, scholars and students would sit for hours, days, or weeks in imposing but uncomfortable reading rooms at Oxford, Heidelberg, or the New York Public Library, peruse, laboriously note direct quotations or paraphrases using pen and paper, and then restructure them in a carefully honed hand or on a typewriter. This took time, which we no longer have. We photocopy or scan material and let computer programs do our thinking for us. A 21st century student who photocopies an assigned reading from *Cell* or *Man* or *Critical Inquiry* could just as easily read the piece in the library, but by copying it, he or she can enjoy it at home, underline the important points, reread it to study for an exam, and file it for future reference (although the chances are good that it will be tossed out at the end of the semester). Students are not going to subscribe to these journals in order to read a single article; indeed, they will not subscribe at all. Thus, photocopying for convenience is not a detriment to potential sales. There is no appreciable difference between a person reading an article in the collection or photocopying it and doing precisely the same thing at home. Patterson and Lindberg (1991) insist that legally, personal copying does not even require reference to the fair use doctrine. Failing to distinguish between consumer (law of personal use) and commercial (law of fair use) applications is, as they observe, an abrogation of both the Constitution's copyright clause as well as the First Amendment. Laura Gasaway and Sarah Wiant (1994), citing Patterson and Lindberg (1991), affirm this point of view, briefly discussing personal use prior to and separate from fair use:

> ...Exceptions [to exclusive rights] provide that the individuals, under certain circumstances, may use, copy, perform, etc., the copyrighted material without the necessity of paying royalties or securing the permission of the owner. Probably the most common of these is one in which there is seldom little discussion and which is not even mentioned in the Act — personal use. Personal use is a private use of a copyrighted work such as reading a literary work for one's own enjoyment or learning. It might also involve sharing the work with a friend or colleague. The hallmark of such personal use is that there is no commercial motive. Personal use has no page length or musical bar restriction; however, it is limited to a single copy for which there is no intention to distribute [25].

Ethically, fair use is not an issue in personal copying, although copyright lawyers might disagree. Publishers, wisely, do not object to this procedure, despite the Copyright Clearing House instructions at the bottom of some pages that are, I suspect, ignored by virtually all individuals.

People may photocopy for personal, non-commercial use, but even libraries are broadly empowered to make copies. Section 108 of the 1976 law, "Limitations on exclusive rights: Reproductions by libraries and archives" (see sidebar) allows an employee to make a single copy or phonorecord of a work in part or in its entirety for purposes of preservation, deposit in another collection, replacement, and patron use both locally or through interlibrary loan. There are many reasonable caveats attached to these user rights, but the result is that collections may reproduce materials to a much greater extent than one might believe based on the general tenor of copyright notices and warnings offered by publishers and vendors.

Attempts on the part of commercial enterprises and organizations to terrorize individuals and libraries into adhering to their interpretations of copy-

---

Copyright Law of 1976: Reproduction by Libraries and Archives (in part)

§108. Limitations on exclusive rights: Reproduction by libraries and archives

(a) Notwithstanding the provisions of section 106, it is not an infringement of copyright for a library or archives, or any of its employees acting within the scope of their employment, to reproduce no more than one copy or phonorecord of a work, or to distribute such copy or phonorecord, under the conditions specified by this section, if—

    (1) the reproduction or distribution is made without any purpose of direct or indirect commercial advantage;

    (2) collections of the library or archives are (i) open to the public, or (ii) available not only to researchers affiliated with the library or archives or with the institution of which it is a part, but also to other persons doing research in a specialized field; and

    (3) the reproduction or distribution of the work includes a notice of copyright.

(b) The rights of reproduction and distribution under this section apply to a copy or phonorecord of an unpublished work duplicated in facsimile form solely for purposes of preservation and security or for deposit for research use in another library or archives of the type described by clause (2) of subsection (a), if the copy or phonorecord reproduced is currently in the collections of the library or archives.

(c) The right of reproduction under this section applies to a copy or phonorecord of a published work duplicated in facsimile form solely for the purpose of replacement of a copy or phonorecord that is damaged, deteriorating, lost, or stolen, if the library or archives has, after a reasonable effort, determined that an unused replacement cannot be obtained at a fair price.

(d) The rights of reproduction and distribution under this section apply to a copy, made from the collection of a library or archives where the user makes his or her request or from that of another library or archives, of no more than one article or other contribution to a copyrighted collection or periodical issue, or to a copy or phonorecord of a small part of any other copyrighted work, if—

    (1) the copy or phonorecord becomes the property of the user, and the library or archives has had no notice that the copy or phonorecord would be used for any purpose other than private study, scholarship, or research; and

    (2) the library or archives displays prominently, at the place where orders are accepted, and includes on its order form, a warning of copyright in accordance with requirements that the Register of Copyrights shall prescribe by regulation.

(e) The rights of reproduction and distribution under this section apply to the entire work, or to a substantial part of it, made from the collection of a library or archives where the user makes his or her request or from that of another library or archives, if the library or archives has first determined, on the basis of a reasonable investigation, that a copy or phonorecord of the copyrighted work cannot be obtained at a fair price, if—

    (1) the copy of the phonorecord becomes the property of the user, and the library or archives has had no notice that the copy or phonorecord would be used for any purpose other than private study, scholarship, or research; and

    (2) the library or archives displays prominently, at the place where orders are accepted, and includes on its order form, a warning of copyright in accordance with requirements that the Register of Copyrights shall prescribe by regulation.

right law by affixing threatening and demanding notices to published works, producing imposing but non-binding dictates in brochures, and bringing court actions, ignore both users' legal rights, as articulated in the Constitution, the fair use doctrine, and section 108, "which specifically authorizes a library to make a single copy of a work for a user on request..." (Patterson & Lindberg, 1991, p. 184) as well as their ethical rights, which supersede fair use.

These remarks assume that an individual or a collection is acting in

Case Study: The Artist

A patron requested some help from Albert Granton, a reference librarian and archivist at a small college. She was compiling a brief biographical catalogue of the work of a famous artist who had donated many valuable materials to Granton's collection. Some of these were published books and articles about his work; others were unpublished notes, diaries, preliminary sketches, and manuscripts.

The requestor, a well-known and respected art historian, was too ill to visit the college, and so she wondered whether Granton could have a student go through a reasonable number of both published and unpublished items, which she specifically cited, photocopy those that seemed relevant to her catalogue, and mail them to her. She promised to return them (uncopied) for destruction after she completed her work.

accordance with some reasonable, non-abusive standard. A student who copies one or two articles from a journal or magazine in order to facilitate learning is acting ethically and legally; were the same student to copy hundreds of articles in order to avoid subscribing or to resell to classmates, then he or she would be guilty of unethical activity and copyright infringement, which is punishable by the courts. More egregious is the reproduction of material in order to avoid subscribing by commercial entities such as corporate libraries or information centers. If a business subscribes to a single copy of an expensive, limited circulation industry newsletter, one that produces income for its owner by tendering esoteric and valuable information or data, then multiple reproductions of this in part or in its entirety in order to disseminate the contents quickly and efficiently to many of the company's employees obviously defeats the very purpose of the newsletter (to earn money for its publisher by offering currently valuable material to subscribers). If this were carried to an extreme, one subscriber could disseminate free copies to hundreds of friends, colleagues, and acquaintances, which would put the publisher out of business. Such activity is blatantly unethical. It is also illegal and that was the finding in the *Pasha* case. In the *Texaco* case, even copying a single journal article (with similar intent) has been found to be illegal (Bielefield and Cheeseman, 1993).

Digital Full Text

Publishers now make substantial numbers of print periodicals in full text available online either through their own systems (Academic Press, for example) or through vendors who gather together thousands of individual magazines and journals from hundreds of disparate sources and offer them in a variety of different packages to subscribers who sign licensing agreements. Gale, which acquired Information Access Corporation and its *InfoTrac* databases, exemplifies this second frequently used method. *InfoTrac* offers collections appropriate for school, public, or academic libraries and an institution or consortium may subscribe to one or all of these databases. The hundreds of individual publishers, who may own the copyright to the articles included in their magazines and journals, obviously offer permission to the vendor (Gale or University Microfilms) to make their current and retrospective materials available to the vendor's subscribers in exchange for some monetary compensation. (The articles' authors, who make all of this extensive and profitable commerce possible, generally do not receive any remuneration from these arrangements.) The library's patrons may then use the vendor's search engine to locate articles on a specific topic. It is at this point that copyright considerations seem to become irrelevant, because a user is permitted to read, print, download, or email a single or a thousand articles. (An email protocol, it should be noted, is available at the conclusion of every *InfoTrac* article.) These processes may take place in a library, but because the databases are mounted on the Internet, an authenticated patron may access them from anywhere in the world. Blanket copyright permission is obviously granted as part of the licensing agreement. (This can be extraordinarily expensive; the state of Minnesota pays almost two million dollars for *InfoTrac* access, which it offers its citizens through public and academic libraries.)

There is no doubt that Internet access to a large collection of full text periodicals is an invaluable boon to students and scholars, but it is necessary to keep in mind that this is a quantitative and not a qualitative change in research possibilities. It is an extraordinary convenience, but nothing more. It guarantees large sums of money to vendors and publishers, but this is apparently inadequate because this latter group is now pushing for pay-per-use schemes in libraries. This would completely abrogate the original intent of copyright, fair use, and the exemptions built into the 1976 copyright law by demanding payment for each item copied. This could apply to print and electronic sources. Legitimate and ethical use of information requires vigilance on the part of librarians and their organizations, otherwise the information industry will commodify and commercialize everything available including government materials, and we will pay dearly for data, as we now pay for bottled water, a development that would have been unthinkable to people just a century ago.

Electronic Reserve

There has never been a problem with traditional academic reserve processes, because libraries generally place a purchased copy of a book or periodical in the reserve section for the quarter or semester in which it is to be used. Alternatively, the instructor or a library employee makes a single copy of an essay or article (which is covered by fair use or the statutory exemptions, by extrapolation) and places it on reserve. (The ALA guidelines for reserve indicate that multiple copies are permissible [Gasaway and Wiant, 1994].) At the completion of the course, the material might be retained by the instructor or destroyed. If additional legal defense were required, as Gasaway and Wiant note, reserve is often considered an "extension of the classroom," which is explicitly mentioned in the fair use section of the 1976 copyright act.

Problems may arise with electronic reserve, since this process entails digitizing books—in part or completely—and periodical articles. The online materials are then made available to the academic community of simultaneous users. Although there is no appreciable difference in the community's actual use of the documents—i.e., the same number of students read the required works during the same period of time; they just do so via electronic rather than traditional means— publishers may object. Some facilities simply digitize, based on statutory exemption; others request permission. As this modality is used more frequently, policies, court cases, and additional legislation will allow a viable solution to evolve.

Interlibrary Loan

Lending materials to another library for the use of a patron who requests a book, copy of a magazine or journal article, etc. is accounted for in the 1976 law, affirmed, and perfectly legal as long as certain reasonable rules are followed. Publishers are aware that their prices are often outlandish, that small and even extensive collections cannot purchase or subscribe to everything, that the primary obligation of a librarian is to connect the user with the requested material, and that publishers insist that freelance authors give up all electronic and future rights to their work without additional compensation (which the Supreme Court recently found to be illegal [Greenhouse, 2001]; the solution, by *The New York Times*, for example, to this decision is not to compensate freelancers, but to extirpate their work from databases, unless they offer their permission to replace their articles). Nevertheless, publishers object strenuously to interlibrary loan (ILL) and would prefer that public and academic libraries charge for this service and then compensate the publisher, who would obviously not share the revenue with the authors. Pat Schroeder, president of the Association of American Publishers, speaking in 2001, shows that little ethical progress has been made by publishers during the past quarter of a century. The bottom line is still compensation:

> We have a very serious issue with librarians.... One library buys one of their journals; they give it to other libraries. [Then those libraries] give it to others... [Albanese, 2001, p. 12].

Music and Audio-Visual Materials

Sheet music is no different than a physics text, literary critique, or philosophy essay: it is published in printed form separately or in a bound volume. It is purchased by individuals, musical groups such as orchestras, and public and academic libraries. Much of what has been noted above applies here as well. And yet, there are some major differences that must affect anyone who applies reasonable ethical principles to its reproduction. Sheet music, in whatever form, is sold in much smaller quantities than books and periodical subscriptions; it produces revenue for its publishers (and the composers) because people wish to perform the music, and each performer requires a score. To allow indiscriminate reproduction, so that each member of a large orchestra can play Mahler's *First Symphony,* would be as unfair as not permitting an individual to make a copy of an anthropology article for personal use. Section 108 confines the limitations on exclusive rights for music, without entirely eliminating them. There are guidelines that can help librarians make equitable decisions, especially in an academic setting: emergencies, scholarly work, or teaching allow for copying as long as many caveats are taken into account. Bielefield and Cheeseman (1993) discuss the guidelines in some detail.

Insofar as copyright is concerned, there is no difference between printed items and orally recorded materials. Indeed, the law specifically exempts phonorecords (and by extrapolation some similar media) from exclusive copyright protection so that libraries may serve their patrons. Once again, however, Section 108 proscribes the exclusive rights limitations concerning most audiovisual productions. Individuals have recorded radio broadcasts since the introduction of reel-to-reel tape recorders early in the last century. This does not seem fair, since one might think that widespread recording would delimit the number of units sold. Nevertheless, hundreds of millions of musical records, tapes, and CDs have been purchased by consumers who have access to all types of recording and burning devices.

VCRs present a similar dilemma. An individual can record a television program, or a borrowed or rented video if one has access to two VCRs or one with dual decks. In the latter case, strict warnings on both documentaries and Hollywood productions offer imprisonment and $50,000 fines for copying, but people often ignore even these dire threats. It is certainly unethical for individuals to borrow recordings and videos from libraries and make copies in order to avoid purchasing them. On the other hand, individuals have every right to record a television program, when they are not at home, view it, and then erase it. Even keeping the tape is not unethical (unless it is a purchasable item). Libraries may record programs, but must erase them after some months have elapsed. Naturally, libraries should no more make multiple copies of recordings, tapes, CDs, videos, or DVDs than they would of books or complete periodicals. All of these items, aimed at the consumer market, are reasonably priced and can be purchased in quantity even for smaller collections. Sheet music and scores and especially audiovisual materials present special problems that must be worked out on an individual basis.

Subverting the Constitutional mandate to further learning by emphasizing the protection of authors' rights is both illegal and unethical, but so too is theft: when individuals or corporations mount CDs or videos on the Internet with the explicit purpose of providing others with a source for recording in order to forestall purchasing, they as well as those who record the material are acting illegally and unethically. Library employees should avoid Napster and its progeny until these systems are sanctioned by the materials' producers.

Concluding Remarks

Some years ago, Kenneth Donald Crews (1990) investigated the copyright policies of a group of major American universities. He found that academics tend to be conservative. Fear of liability suits result in the creation of strict policies that proscribe fair use and inhibit the free flow of information, even though the law may be interpreted so as to allow users broader, fuller access. This attitude obviously limits an institution's ability to fulfill its pedagogical purpose. Ironically, the Association of Research Libraries (Bruwelheide, 1995), whose members probably produced the policies that Crews examined, counters this misguided approach by insisting, in a series of principles, that "copyright exists for the public good" (113), i.e., to promote learning; fair use of all formats must be maintained; collections must be allowed to utilize technology to preserve material; licenses should not usurp fair use; librarians should educate patrons;

government information should not be subject to copyright; and authors should be compensated for their work. This is a fair, judicious, and ethical approach to a difficult situation, although publishers and their attorneys undoubtedly view these remarks very differently.

I can do no better than to conclude this chapter with two incisive comments. Patterson and Lindberg (1991) observe that "Charity is not an inborn trait, and the fact that a free-market system makes a virtue of necessity is no cause for society to forfeit the purpose of copyright (the promotion of learning) in favor of its function (to protect the author's right to publish)" (p. 238). And so, "Professors, university administrators, librarians, and document services personnel must remain diligent and willing to assert their rights in order to advance the production of knowledge via the free flow of information" (Trosow, 2001, p. 54).

11

Information Ethics

Sentience and knowledge are concomitants. All zoological entities process information and act upon it. Even an amoeba knows some things, learns, modifies its behavior, and passes on its genes. The more a bear, raccoon, dolphin, or chimpanzee knows, the more likely it is that it will survive; what it does not know may prove terminally harmful. Hominids, like other animals, acted instinctively, learned, mastered their environment, and prospered. Early *homo sapiens* added two extraordinary advantages to the typical animal's armamentarium. They could speak and thereby communicate even complex and abstract thoughts and they could think: they were able to process data and information in a rational, logical manner, draw conclusions, and act upon them. Thus it was possible for puny, sensorily delimited, defenseless mammals to hold their own against much larger, stronger, and better equipped animals. They learned about agriculture, edible creatures, tracking, navigation, fire, clothing, weaponry, medicinals, construction, and thousands of other pragmatic applications. Those who learned best and thereby accumulated useful knowledge were most successful. Information was as important to our distant ancestors as it is to the information society. We just need more, immediately, wherever we happen to be. We master data and information, turn it into real knowledge, prolong lives or build more efficient bombs, but we do not know what to do with the senile nonogenarians filling our nursing homes or the enemies who provoke us. Neither our moral sense nor our ethical sophistication has kept pace with our extraordinary technological prowess. Information is power; it is also overwhelming, confusing, and harmful.

I first proposed the phrase "information ethics" (IE) almost 15 years ago (Hauptman, 1988), in the opening pages of *Ethical Challenges in Librarianship.* At about the same time, Rafael Capurro (1988) in Germany came up with "Informationsethik." Four years later, I founded the *Journal of Information Ethics* (Hauptman, 1992). The term is now used unbiquitously in innumerable disciplines. IE is an applied, extremely broad, encompassing subdiscipline of ethics that takes all informational areas under its wing. Thus, for example, medical, legal, journalism, computer science, and business ethics, in this context, are merely subsets of IE.

Information ethics concerns itself with the production, dissemination, storage, retrieval, security, and application of information within an ethical context. There are many apposite examples of ethical problems presented by the mere collection of information. Consider the Nazi experiments that codified knowledge concerning temperature alterations in the human body. This data was derived from concentration camp victims under duress. Laypersons, ethicists, and even some interested scientists hold that this material should not be utilized. On the other hand, one could argue that since people suffered dramatically to produce this knowledge, it honors them to apply it in order to better humankind. It is very difficult to decide which of these perspectives is valid; that is why this is an irresolvable dilemma for some people. Martha Smith (2001) has created and refined a useful taxonomy for IE, most recently restructured as global information justice (GIJ). Information ethics can be divided into five broad categories— ownership, access, privacy, security, and community— that cover virtually all contingencies, some of which are not discussed here. For a fuller treatment covering computer ethics, peer review, fraud, whistle blowing, and other topics, see my still useful bibliographic essay on information ethics (Hauptman, 1999).

Ownership

Individual and corporate creators of information are ethically responsible for the manner in which it is derived and produced. This means that in a civilized society, one directed and oriented by ethical mandates (rather than mere legalities), animals should not be tortured to confirm yet again that tobacco smoke has a deleterious effect on the lungs or that abrasive creams and powders do indeed harm the eye. Human subjects must be treated with care and deference, not abused physically, mentally, or emotionally nor taken advantage of because of situational, linguistic, financial, or mental incapacity, i.e., informed consent must be truly informed. Feminist research theory insists that there are certain areas into which humans should not delve. Although this runs counter to the scientific spirit of inquiry, it would benefit humankind if we avoided the creation of ever bigger, faster, and more lethal armaments. Data and information are often derived through unacceptable practices. The ultimate owners of the material should not shut their eyes to the preliminary steps that bring it into existence.

Given the nature of capitalist society reinforced by patent, trademark, and copyright protection, one might, reasonably enough, think that the ownership of a created or produced entity, whether physical or informational, whether mere data or more sophisticated and codified knowledge, would be clearcut and absolute. But as it happens this is not the case. Data that logically appear to belong legally and ethically to a specific person actually does not.

For example, in *Who Owns Information?*, Anne Wells Branscomb (1994) provides a revelatory overview of the ownership of basic information including one's name, address, telephone number, medical history, image, and electronic messages, as well as government data. Although some protection against the misuse or abuse of this information exists (for example, it is illegal to forge another person's name on a check, one can pay for an unlisted phone number, and the commercial exploitation of a person's image is illegal), companies inundate us with annoying written and telephonic pleas to purchase, rent, lease, or subscribe to their products; virtually everyone except the patient has access to one's medical records; an embarrassing photograph can appear on the front page of *The National Enquirer* or *USA Today*, if it constitutes legitimate news; and employers scan, read, peruse, or archive email messages and may fire an employee who says something untoward. Here we are dealing with data that ostensibly belongs to the individual.

Government information is produced at the taxpayers' expense and so it too, in a sense, belongs to each citizen, although as information has become more valuable, it has been commodified, and commercial firms now repackage government data and sell it to individuals, organizations, and governmental bodies. Although information has always had value, it was frequently given away for nothing, even in the recent past, as advice, through mass media offerings, and in government publications.

Today, much can be gleaned from Internet home pages, but Fritz Machlup's (1962) detailed analysis of knowledge production, the shift to postindustrial society in which what we know is the controlling economic force, and the resulting commodification of information, allow those who produce, own, or assemble data and information to sell them to those willing to pay. Internet material that seems to be free is not. It often appears on one's screen because a producer has paid a search engine service, thus altering its objective value. Viewers may suffer the necessity of inundating advertisements, and when an information provider is potentially or actually successful, a charge for the service is certain to follow.

Providers of esoteric information, including doctors, lawyers, stock brokers, money managers, and business advisors, are among our most highly respected and remunerated workers. Even teachers are honored, although their compensation lags behind other professionals. Those who own information or are empowered by what they know have a social responsibility to offer their knowledge at a fair market value; when professionals or corporations charge hundreds of times what their service or product is actually worth, they are acting unethically.

Professional knowledge — what a doctor, lawyer, or architect knows — as well as purely commercial data and information are among our most valuable assets. That is why they can be tendered in exchange for extraordinary payments. It defies common sense that a battery of lawyers should receive half of a paralyzed or poisoned victim's court-awarded compensation or that a publisher could convince a librarian to pay $16,000 a year for a journal subscription. These information abuses throw microeconomies out of kilter and ultimately have a detrimental effect on society. A few individuals or corporations reap unwarranted profits at the expense of the consumer. One need only consider the 16th century Dutch tulip craze to realize that, analogously, information exploitation must eventually become counterproductive. I do not mean to imply that the commodification of data and information is entirely negative, but the abuses associated with it are. Ownership, especially of data and information that can help to truly improve our lives, entails a commitment to act in a socially responsible manner.

A pharmaceutical company may sell its beneficial medicinals at a fair price, but it should also make these products available in Third World countries at reduced rates. It can make an excellent profit from a frequently sold antibiotic, but it must also continue to produce orphan drugs and offer them at a reasonable cost for the sufferers who require them. Considering only a pecuniary responsibility to owners or stockholders is no longer a tenable philosophy. Today, the bottom line encompasses more than it did during capitalism's exploitative period. Socially uncaring companies that abuse information ownership are no longer tolerated; when enough consumers boycott their products, they will go out of business. Thus, acting ethically makes good business sense. Perhaps that is why some corporations are now hiring full time ethicists and paying them enormous salaries.

Case Study: The Formula

A large, European pharmaceutical company has a stringently controlling patent on an inexpensive drug whose single application cures a horrific disease that is endemic in many of the world's tropical areas. The company offers its treatment at many hundreds of times the production cost. This is not a problem in wealthier countries, where people can easily afford to purchase the pills. But in poverty stricken sub–Saharan or Asian lands, the victims do not have the money to buy the single dosage. Social organizations have pressured the company's managers, but they refuse to discount their products. Now a small concern in India has begun to produce a generic version of the drug and is offering it in Third World countries at a few pennies above cost. The European conglomerate is threatening to sue.

A generation ago, it would have been inconceivable that we would patent genetic structures, but now this occurs as a matter of course. Even an individual subject's or patient's genetic line may be controlled by a researcher. Information is power. What could be more powerful than the manipulation of genetic information to improve offspring? Corn is more resistant to pests, tomatoes maintain their flavor for longer periods, and humans are healthier. Eugenics creates a better person, not prone to diabetes, cystic fibrosis, Tay-Sachs disease, or sickle cell anemia. No one can argue against these improvements. But ownership of genetic information is fraught with peril. Employment, insurance availability, social standing, and quality of life all may suffer, if an unscrupulous person abuses this confidential knowledge.

Finally, it is obvious that general and especially proscribed information can be used to cause harm. One may know something about a business or individual that if broadly disseminated could destroy the company or the person's career. A greedy individual could hold others hostage to the information, make demands or threaten to reveal what he or she knows. This is often illegal and always unethical. Proprietary information acquired on the job should be protected even after moving to a competing firm. Sensitive agencies such as the FBI, CIA, or NSA require employees to promise not to reveal anything they know for five years after they leave. In cases in which operatives' lives may be in danger, it would be unethical to ever indicate names, places, or situations.

Information ownership entails concomitant responsibilities. If one maintains what one knows privately, then it is permissible to distort as one wishes. But if an individual or corporation becomes an information provider, if one chooses to disseminate data or information, then it is incumbent upon the provider to make certain that no purposeful or inadvertent errors have slipped into what one offers in articles, books, or on Web sites. The comparatively recent trend to propagandize or dissimulate is unwarranted. We expect disinformation to pervade totalitarian societies such as North Korea, but purposeful and continual disinformation emanating from governmental agencies in France, Australia, or the United States is reprehensible. It may confuse the enemy, if there happens to be one in attendance, but it is especially harmful to the country's integrity as well as to the citizens it should be nurturing and protecting.

Access

In the past, anyone in the Western world could walk into a small or large public library or a public or even private research collection and have access to all of humankind's knowledge. This is still the case, although now one must know how to manipulate computer systems; additionally, some academic institutions may not allow unaffiliated patrons to use certain databases. Those individuals who are interested in convenient information access or in furthering their children's education will purchase computers and pay for Internet access in their homes, unless, of course, they cannot afford the hardware, software, connection time, paper, and ink cartridges; they may also balk at the misinformation, propaganda, blasphemy, hate, and pornography that the Web makes so accessible, and therefore refuse to participate. Thus, a large segment of the First World's population is overwhelmed with information, whereas a smaller group's access is delimited or nonexistent. And it is imperative to keep in mind that once one leaves the developed countries, Internet access is comparatively limited. Some nations have few if any providers or servers; some delimit access for political or religious reason; and most of the people in Tibet, Chad, or El Salvador do not have the disposable income to purchase a computer, even if it is physically possible to connect to a phone line and service provider.

A decade or two ago, medical schools in countries such as Uganda were unable to afford expensive journal subscriptions and so Makarere University's periodical collection was ten years behind the times. A poor economy and a lack of corporate altruism hindered access to the latest medical discoveries. If one had suggested to representatives of Elsevier, Springer Verlag, and John Wiley that they offer 90 percent discounts on their scientific and medical journals to Third World subscribers, they would have found the idea laughable. After all, these publishers are in business to earn a profit, not to provide inexpensive or free medical information to Nigerians or Bolivians. But during the summer of 2001, things changed. A consortium of these very presses as well as other medical journal publishers agreed to allow Third World academics free or very inexpensive access to electronic versions of some 1,000 publications (Manning, 2001). Although the exceptionally high subscription rates that the First World's libraries pay for these periodicals will subsidize their dissemination to poorer countries, this is precisely what is ethically required: making information accessible to those who otherwise would be deprived.

Theorists, politicians, and even laypersons have touted the benefits of cyberspace and the communication revolution it instigated. People can now interact with each other through web pages, listservs, email, bulletin boards, chat groups, instant messaging, and even free telephone calls. The result of all of these exchanges is broader access to opinions, data, and information that is supposed to increase the general intelligence level, and offer citizens more material for informed decisions and thereby improve the democratic process through which we thrive economically and humanly. This does appear to be a reasonable analysis and to some degree it is probably true. Concomitantly, instead of doing something constructive, like reading Franklin's *Autobiography* or *The Federalist Papers*, people waste time: much of what passes for communication is gossip or gibberish, the type of small talk in which adolescents engage. Alexander Stille (2001) points out that discussants who agree reinforce each other's perspective, which then solidifies into a more extreme position; this results in fragmented communities.

The Internet also allows scam artists, criminals, child abusers, and hatemongers easy access to their victims. Widely disseminated misinformation concerning minorities or other populations who are generally despised (e.g., Americans in Iran, capitalists in Cuba) with the intent to incite hatred perverts the democratic ethos that cyberspace ostensibly nurtures. The universal harm that has been instigated through cyberpropaganda in places like Israel, Ireland, the Balkans, Russia, and the United States is probably greater than all of the democratic benefits that have accrued to potential voters, incipient activists, and political revolutionaries.

There are those who defend the extreme position that all information should be universally accessible without any charge. All the data and information mounted on Web pages or housed on commercial servers and offered to subscribers, sometimes for very large fees, should be freely accessible. All of the text, images, software, video, music, multimedia, and other materials that creators and producers have assembled ostensibly belong to the people and they should have free access to them. The fact that the naive or dishonest actually implement this program and take material that does not belong to them apparently has a palliative effect on those who normally respect property and copyright. The idea seems to be that if millions of people are stealing software or music then it is acceptable to do so. Although most of these people would not steal a book or magazine from Brentano's or Rizzoli's, they often advocate the dissolution of copyright, which would allow for the reproduction of anything anyone happens to mount on the Web. Thus, universal accessibility would become a virtual reality. Until this occurs with the imprimatur of the putative owners, hackers and crackers will continue to help themselves (and others) to whatever is desired, including proscribed and confidential information such as social security, credit card, and bank account data.

Privacy

There are very few issues on which a diverse population of almost 300 million people can agree, but the invasion of privacy is one of them. In the earliest surveys dealing with privacy issues, only a small percentage of those queried indicated that they were really concerned. As more people were hurt, as the media publicized scams, fraud, financial loss, identity theft, and insurance and employment problems, and as privacy encroachments came to include the abuse of genetic data, the public's interest increased, so that now a high percentage of those questioned indicate that this is an issue of grave concern. It is most pressing — theoretically, for those who care about civil liberties and democratic rights and, practically, for individuals who have had the bad luck to suffer some harm at the hands of an oppressive employer, insurer, government bureaucrat, con man, or identity thief.

Consider that just a few years ago, security or surveillance cameras could be found in banks, casinos, and some larger stores. Today, these devices are ubiquitous in business environments, at academic institutions, on roadways, and on the streets of big cities. For example, at first one had to struggle to locate the 20 or 30 cameras that surveyed the streets of Manhattan. Today, there are thousands of these devices aimed at citizens and tourists innocently wandering around Manhattan. Some of these cameras are operated by the government, but most are owned by corporations that ostensibly employ them to protect their business interests. Thus, any person walking in New York is tracked and recorded, and naturally the curious may abuse this bizarre privilege and aim their cameras into people's offices or apartments. A democratic society should not have to put up with such blatant privacy intrusions predicated on the possibility that someone might commit a crime so heinous that it warrants continuous and invasive surveillance of the general public. The innocent should not be punished for the misdeeds of a few barbarians. Surveillance of public environments, monitoring of business interactions, and spying on one's neighbors at the behest of a benighted government are unacceptable activities in a democratic society. That all of these procedures are now part of our lives is neither a warrant nor a mandate for their continued exercise. What is apparently appropriate or acceptable in China and North Korea or at airlines and car rental or trucking companies should not become the norm in enlightened environments.

Just a few thousand cases of identity theft were reported in 1999; this unpleasant crime increased dramatically in 2000; and, horrifically, some 500,000 instances were predicted for 2001. Identity theft is especially pernicious, because it encroaches on one's privacy financially, but it affects the victim physically and psychologically as well. In some cases, it might not come to light for years, and although a person is not legally liable, one's credit rating, good name, and mental well being can all be devastated. We trade security for convenience: telephonic and various forms of electronic commerce make it very easy for the dishonest to relieve us of our money. Social security and credit card numbers, mothers' secret maiden names, academic, medical, and criminal records, and other sensitive data are all available to those who are either able to manipulate computers or willing to pay an information broker for his or her services. Some information is protected, encrypted, or secreted, but much of it is readily and legally available.

Politicians work at our behest and many state and federal legislators continue to attempt to pass laws that protect our privacy. But in this case, legislation and harsh penalties for infractions are not enough. There are always those who are willing to risk punishment because of potential gain or because it is gratifying for a hacker to succeed in subverting the system. And tracking children and adults for marketing purposes as they visit Web sites, though disconcerting and unethical, is perfectly legal. Thus, it is up to each individual to make certain that his or personal data and information is protected. Despite all of the discussion, legal imbroglios, and new legislation, our privacy is under attack. Once it is gone, it will be impossible to retrieve it.

Security

We have a right to be secure in our person, homes, and technological extensions. We must protect this right and ourselves by controlling the physical equipment that we engage; this includes, for example, automobiles, telephones, copy machines, and especially computers, systems, and networks. Once the physical aspect of our tools is protected, we must control access to them. We do not want counterfeiters using our copiers to produce currency nor do we want crackers breaking into our files in order to manipulate, forge, or steal. And, naturally, whatever we call up from the Web must have integrity, something that was guaranteed, at least to a limited extent, in the print world, where the editing process ostensibly eliminated falsity, but which is sorely lacking in cyberspace. Consider the simple case of Marcus Arnold, a 15 year old adolescent who offered legal advice on a web site. Even after participants discovered that he was a child with no legal training, they continued to seek his advice (Lewis, 2001).

Because this is not a technical manual, detailed suggestions concerning credit card usage, banking, medical records, sensitive data, cookies, encryption, viruses, trojan horses, firewalls, and other pertinent items are not addressed here. Adam Cohen (2001) reviews nine major security problems (e.g., unintentional revelation, stolen data, fake websites, spying) and offers some reasonable advice on how to protect against disaster (e.g., install firewalls, take care, opt out, encrypt). Many computer users are either naive or unconcerned, but even the sophisticated and knowledgeable sometimes reveal unencrypted credit card data to pay for some trifle, offer personal information in exchange for a meaningless lagniappe, or fail to update their protective utilities or guard against the incursions that accompany attachments. Until security is taken seriously, people will continue to be hurt, sometimes seriously.

Community

For some thinkers, information ethics has evolved into global information justice (GIJ), a more powerful concept with broader applicability and usefulness. Since information is our single most important resource, a necessity for acquiring and maintaining even life's basic necessities, it is unethical, i.e., unjust, to deprive people anywhere of whatever they need to know in order to prosper. GIJ insists that information and its concomitant technologies be used in a responsible and caring way. Smith (2001) believes that a communal approach to information justice is mandatory. Thus, education and individualized, multicultural development rather than universal homogeneity enhances community which in turn fosters the positive growth of each person. But affirming a communal or communitarian attitude does not imply that some people must suffer in order that others may prosper, nor does it mean that anyone must sacrifice basic human rights, privacy, for example, in order to protect the community. One may care about local or global neighbors without becoming a cog or serf.

True community and information justice is thwarted when, for example, the law mandates that federal web sites must be accessible to the disabled, but many agencies' sites fail to accommodate these people (Bridis and Simpson, 2001). Information justice is bizarrely perverted when the Internet is used to purvey misleading, malicious, or false accusations against specific groups of people based on their nationality, ethnicity, religion, or race. No one insists that everyone love all six billion human beings, but using technology to purvey hate that results in mental anguish or physical harm to people around the world is not merely unethical; it is an egregious evil. Although censorship is anathema and unacceptable, prosecuting hate mongers for inciting harm is not.

Conclusion

In addition to its practical or financial value, information, according to Mark Alfino and Linda Pierce (2001), also has a social or moral nature. When corporations insist that tobacco is an innocuous product or when studios pay people to offer testimonials for their films, we expect no less. But when Nobel Prize winner Rigobertu Menchu distorts the truth for effect, when Pulitzer Prize and National Book Award winning historian Joseph Ellis misleads a generation of students into believing that he was a Viet Nam veteran, when Binjamin Wilkomerski's Holocaust memoir turns out to be fictive, or when a scientific icon like Louis Pasteur is shown to have been dishonest, their discourse is sullied. We trust those who appear to honor truth and when they disappoint us, the moral nature of the information they purvey is desecrated.

Like technology, information may take on a life of its own and direct a course of action for those who mistakenly believe that they are leading. Since information is power, the life blood of the contemporary world, it behooves us to produce and apply it in acceptable and caring ways. Nevertheless, Bernd Frohmann (2000) insists that "there is no information ethics" (p. 434); by this rhetorical turn he means that ethical consideration concerning information is basically the same as ethical consideration of all other possibilities, an argument analogous to the one articulated by opponents of, say, computer ethics. I can but repeat that traditional deontological and consequentialist thinking are more than adequate for our current needs and so we do not require a new ethical superstructure to solve our problems, but IE allows us to view the informational world in its entirety and make decisions that are more encompassing than those that are discipline specific. IE offers the advantage of a holistic, interdisciplinary perspective, which an Internet connected world demands. As Martha Montague Smith noted in 1998, "In less than ten years, information ethics has grown within library and information science and has emerged from this field into international discourse on professionalism and public policy" (356).

It has taken more than a century for ethical considerations to become an integral part of the pedagogical experience of information workers and this has occurred in only some fora. Most educators continue to believe that hands-on skills using *AACR2*, reference books, computers, and software programs are far more important than understanding ethical theory or even acting correctly. Catholic University offered an early course in apposite ethical considerations and the University of Pittsburgh's information ethics class is both popular and successful. The Pittsburgh IE web site (http://www.sis.pitt.edu/~ethics) is especially informative. The International Center for Information Ethics also maintains a useful site at http://v.hbi-stuttgart.de/~capurro/icie-index.html.

In 1975, Edward O. Wilson published *Sociobiology: The New Synthesis.* The first 26 chapters of this seminal study deal with animal sociobiology; it is only in the final chapter that Wilson discusses the biological foundation of human behavior. Thus, there is some precedent for the type of extrapolation derived from empirical and experiential study I have offered here.

12

Why Ethics Matters

I wander into the reference area at a major academic research institution. I notice that the unappealingly crowded and messy information desk is empty, but that there are two librarians sitting next to each other, shoulders touching, at the reference desk. They are staring into space or reading; I walk over and ask about their desk coverage. The woman informs me that she only works part-time so she does not know; she gets up and begins to consult a schedule. The man silently hands me a sheet of paper. I try again. This time I wonder how many students attend this enormous university. The man answers, "I don't know." "You don't know how many students you have!" "No. You might contact the regents." I walk away, confused and disgusted.*

Ethics matters because it allows us to function in a humane and socially equitable manner without the control of a casuistic or demagogic legal system. But apparently it does not matter very much to librarians. A quarter of a century ago, when I published "Professionalism or Culpability" (Hauptman, 1976), only a handful of pertinent publications existed and most of them dealt with etiquette. As the general social ethos has changed, as individuals, business people, bureaucrats, and legislators have begun to consider actions in an ethical context, so too have information

---

*I had this encounter in the spring of 2001 at the main library of a major research university. Incompetence and an uncaring attitude are tantamount to ethical breaches. These people should be doing something other than "helping" patrons.

specialists turned their attention to ethical matters; but their scholarly commitment appears to be rather proscribed. A search of four concepts on the *Library Literature* database for the period 1980–2000 turned up the following results: service — 7,015 items; Internet — 6,872 items; selection — 2,234 items; ethics — 726 items. The Internet did not exist just a few years ago, whereas ethical considerations have been guiding human beings, professionals, and information specialists for millennia. Nevertheless, only 726 separate items are available in the literature during the past two decades and many of these are ephemeral comments. I next turned my attention to the monographic literature. In a large library science collection (the LC "Z" classification), I randomly selected 50 volumes and checked the indexes; only six contained the term "ethics." Generally, we do try to act correctly, but we often fail. We only discuss our failures occasionally.

Values

We fail to do the right thing because our values are merely theoretical constructs that do not warrant serious consideration and practical implementation. Some years ago, Michael Gorman (2000) published an insightful consideration of eight values that offer foundational support to librarianship: stewardship, service, intellectual freedom, rationalism, literacy and learning, equity of access, privacy, and democracy are the concepts that Gorman believes undergird all that we do. As he observes, others might have created a slightly different list, but most thinkers would include these criteria in any serious discussion of the values that lend meaning to librarianship. If we honored these, incorporated them fully and wholeheartedly into our individual and professional belief systems, acted upon them as if our lives depended upon their implementation, and inculcated them in colleagues, peers, and patrons, then ethical commitment and concomitant actions would follow naturally and completely. But as it happens in the real world, these are ideal values that we discuss at conferences and workshops, briefly consider in the literature, but often fail to fully respect or implement. We have, for example, a responsibility to protect the physical and intellectual artifacts of the past, we discuss preservation in articles and at conferences, but we lose tens of thousands of volumes each year to thieves and vandals, purposely destroy hard copy, weed, and fail to maintain older technologies. Lamentably, we are not very good stewards of the material entrusted to us.

We serve, but begrudgingly. I am well aware that there are thousands of dedicated public service information professionals who work long and hard in order to help and satisfy patrons often with no reward other than the satisfaction that accrues from a successful endeavor. Some of us do more with no tangible reward than a salesperson may do for a commission or bonus. Nevertheless, librarians are often less than helpful, uncaring, and perform their duties in a perfunctory manner. It is not necessary to continue with this exercise, since similar things could be said for most of the remaining concepts. Gorman's values are our values; it just happens that it is sometimes inconvenient to further them in the real world. We do the best we can under the circumstances and excuse the failures.

Guidance

Guy St. Clair (1997) lists five characteristics of the ethical information services manager: integrity, humaneness, professionalism, fairness, and excellence of service apply to all people in the information fields, and indeed to any service professional. These attributes are comprehensible and undoubtedly acceptable to most information workers, who presumably attempt to live up to these ideals. Surprisingly, many fail. Human beings are often dishonest, inefficient, ineffective, and unreliable; we mistreat each other, because in pragmatic situations the ends ostensibly justify the means; professionals are often disrespected, especially in an academic environment and so we may act unprofessionally; although we spend much of our time convincing ourselves that we are judicious and nurturing, we are frequently unfair and care little for real justice; finally, we abdicate in favor of mediocrity. This is a harsh assessment, but it is probably accurate and a telling comment, not just on librarians but on many professionals. On the other hand, if we could live up to these five attributes, we would be better human beings and more successful as information providers.

Richard Rubin and Thomas Froehlich (1996) offer some excellent advice on how to nurture ethical commitment. The library organization should support a committed board, training, and the ethically aware, and establish a policy, *inter alia*; the profession must offer a code, training, and advice; and the individual is admonished to act in a responsible, truthful manner and to affirm equal access. Rubin and Froehlich's taxonomy is complex and replete, but this summary provides a fair overview of their suggestions. If the profession took ethical commitment as seriously as it does faster computers, technological gadgetry, superfluous software, and expensive data bases, we would still be faced with difficult challenges, but we would also solve some problems or ameliorate some conditions.

The ALA Code provides a good example of what is wrong with our commitment to ethics. It is an old but often revised document; many caring people have spent lots of time honing it so that it presumably approximates the possible. And yet, it has been severely criticized because it rhetorically exhorts but provides no reason for adherence. It does not jibe with reality, and information workers follow its tenets at their convenience. We scrupulously avoid conflicts of interest, but concomitantly ignore the requirement to avoid censoring; we strive to serve with excellence, but confuse our own perspectives with the profession's. Codes, rules, regulations, and even laws do not create or foster an ethical environment; a true commitment on the part of the organization and its individual members is mandatory if we are to operate fairly, and offer all patrons and clients the service that they deserve while avoiding social harm.

Excuses

Banks McDowell (2000) claims that professionals are no longer willing to take responsibility for their actions. Instead, they excuse themselves. It is obvious that offering an excuse for an action should not always be construed negatively; sometimes an excuse functions as a legitimate explanation. More often, though, it is an attempt to shift responsibility and accountability so that they devolve elsewhere. McDowell creates an extensive taxonomic structure, first of ethical and then of legal excuses. In the former group fall ignorance, transference, other obligations, pressure, equipment, unfortunate result, kindness, irrationality, victim, and non-illegality. In the latter category we find accident, mistake, lack of intent, self-defense, victim's responsibility, fraud, duress, consent, and transfer of responsibility. There may be instances when legal excuses are applied in librarianship, but usually aberrations involve ethical breaches and attempts to excuse them to oneself and to others. It is easy to see, for example, how virtually any failure can be ascribed to ignorance; how we cannot help someone at a particular moment, because we must do something else; how malfunctioning equipment is at fault rather than the librarian or technician; or how, out of kindness, we might attempt to save patrons from extra work by leading them to an online, full-text source and forget to mention that there are thousands of other (more appropriate) literary journals, an omission that ultimately may harm the work these people are doing.

Patrons do not ask much of us; we are not removing tumors nor defending death-row prisoners. Marilyn Christianson (2001) rightly castigates the profession for refusing to accommodate users, who become frustrated and angry because the rules are so inflexible, the equipment so unreliable, the stock of books and journals so negligible, the resources so inadequate, and workers' attitudes so unhelpful. Christianson insists that patrons have legitimate complaints and defends their right to send email, access popular computer books, not pay exorbitant charges for poor copies, and avoid irascible employees. Excuses are counterproductive.

Principles and Consequences

Ethics matters because it allows us to implement our divergent values in a non-coercive environment. When obligations or commitments clash, we can attempt to solve problems without undue external legal pressure. Adherence to principle allows us to defend even those perspectives that we know are false or nonsensical. At first glance, this would appear to be an unwarranted position, but the extirpation of what John Swan (1998) terms "untruth" has two dire consequences. It sets a precedent for delimiting intellectual freedom through censorious activity and it expunges points of view to which others adhere and that might turn out to be true despite the current perspective. Protecting untruth is the antithesis of the point made above that scholarly communication demands the correction of errors and the retraction of falsified, fabricated, or plagiarized material. This dilemma, created by two clashing principles, is soluble: labeling of some sort would allow librarians to alert patrons and thus permit readers to make a decision without infringing on their intellectual freedom.

Ethics matters because it helps us to stand up to peers who only care about immediate consequences and who are therefore willing to subjugate principles in order to placate politicians, parents, fanatics, and other shortsighted people who want to sacrifice freedom in order to eliminate material they happen to find offensive. We know that censorship is unacceptable but sometimes defend filtering because it saves us from howling protesters, lawsuits, and loss of federal funds. We react negatively when we are asked to remove Dante, Hawthorne, Salinger, or Blume from the shelves, but we listen attentively when David Burt (1997) defends filtering in the pages of *American Libraries*. An ethical commitment to intellectual freedom would allow us to reject his specious arguments, and to at least attempt to convince those who wish to protect their children from pornography that thought control is not the best solution, because in the long run it causes irreparable harm.

When libraries are sued for not filtering (Library, 1999), professionals and organizations must come to their aid. When pornography ostensibly creates a hostile work environment (Kornblum, 2000), the courts must affirm our Constitutional right to intellectual freedom and information access regardless of how it might offend some employees. Many solutions to this problem exist; no group of puritanical librarians should be allowed to superimpose their personal preferences on the information seeking ability of patrons. Consider that the feminist Andrea Dworkin fought a hard battle to implement intellectually repressive ordinances in Indianapolis and Minneapolis, with some brief success. Ironically, this attempt to silence others ultimately failed, but Canadian authorities decided that her novel, *Intercourse,* was unacceptable reading matter and so it was banned.

Ethics matters because we must not always take the easy or even legal path. Despite the passage of half a century, when we discover that our collections, including the Library of Congress, contain material stolen by Nazi hooligans and looters and brought to the United States by American military personnel (Sanger, 2001), we must return it. This painful situation is analogous to cases in which museum officials or even private individuals discover that their prized paintings belong to someone else. During the seventies or eighties, it may have been unusual for a curator or director to hand over the disputed works, but the ethos has changed and the return of these stolen artifacts is no longer an unusual occurrence.

Ethics insists that we take a stand against unreasonable publishers who inundate us with useless, repetitive, or expensive monographs, cloned, extrapolated, or exorbitantly priced journals, and superfluous and glitzy media products. Every dissertation submitted at American or European universities does not deserve publication, and we should be wary of publishers who offer thousands of unedited volumes each year. Even *Nature,* one of the world's premier scientific publications, has decided to produce innumerable offspring including *Nature Genetics, Nature Immunology, Nature Neuroscience, Nature Reviews Genetics,* ad infinitum. We should fight to eliminate the dual pricing system that allows journals to reap extraordinary profits. *Ethics and Behavior,* for example, has an annual subscription rate for individuals of $35, but institutions must pay $360.

Ethics can help. If we adhere to traditional values, we will not be seduced into believing that when situations change so must our commitment; we do not require different ethical principles, mandates, or structures. As Mary Bushing (1993) insists, we should not "redefine ethics for hard times" (p. 50): just as it is not okay to steal merely because one is homeless, so it is not ethically acceptable to manipulate principles because publishers are greedy or budgets are constrained. Principled thinking allows us to see through and beyond the convoluted and manipulative rhetoric that helps philosophers present convincing but misleading defenses of censorship (Fricke, Mathiesen, & Fallis, 2000). If there are more fundamental rights than freedom of thought, then anyone, naturally, can cite those rights when attempting to control what students may read in a class, what libraries may collect, and what Americans may access on the Internet. There is indeed a dichotomy between the principles that undergird American librarianship and our daily activities, but the disparities are not ascribable to fallibility and the fear that one might make a mistake. Rather, it is due to our inability to adhere to principles, as well as the tendency on the part of caring and committed people to take the path of least resistance; we operate under what I have termed the ethic of convenience.

If some scholars and practitioners wish to extend ethical conjecture and mandates into every area of our professional lives, create a casuistic code that controls us as lawyers are constrained, Guy Marco (1996) argues that ethical considerations only apply in a limited number of areas. He blithely dismisses general moral behavior, information ethics, and the "ethics of librarianship." He apparently was not thinking analogically, otherwise he would have to eliminate medical and legal ethics as well. Whereas most thinkers broaden their nets too expansively, Marco bizarrely rejects issues such as competence, censorship, and privacy, and homes in on just four areas: Selection, reference, equal treatment, and profit taking are the only appropriate venues for ethical consideration in librarianship, and everything else is redundant. Many of the subtle but important issues raised in this study are out of scope.

Sometimes, ordinary citizens are more perceptive and knowledgeable than scholars and professionals. While some thinkers offer a philosophical foundation for censorious activity or do not believe that censorship is an ethical problem at all, the people of conservative Holland, Michigan, voted against a proposal to filter the Internet. But ironically, the library sanctions a system that requires a professional to precisely monitor and control what patrons may view, download, or print (Bradsher, 2000).

When Ethics Fails

Richard Severson (1995) argues that all librarians should learn more about ethics because we have lost the tradition of ethical reflection, because technology is confusing, and because we are professionals. But even if all librarians were fully committed to ethical action, even if we could all agree that censorship is evil, that information should be free, and that reference personnel should warn users that some material is unreliable or riddled with errors (which we cannot), we would still have major problems, since much of the unacceptable activity occurs on the part of patrons, students, Internet users, and other laypersons. Education, moral suasion, pledges, coercion, and threats may alter negative behavior on the part of some irresponsible people, but there will always be those who choose to annoy, harass, hack, crack, vandalize, stalk, or steal.

For more than 25 years, I have insisted that we must commit ourselves to an ethical infrastructure (including ALA mandates, professional obligations, and individual considerations), act accordingly, and assume responsibility for our behavior. But as society has become more dependent on information and as more information, including private and confidential data, has become more accessible, I have realized that individual ethical commitment is inadequate to the task at hand. This is ironic, because Deborah Johnson (1997) reaches precisely the opposite conclusion. She argues that technological devices such as firewalls can only provide minimal protection for computer systems (and the data and information they contain), since presumably someone will eventually figure out a way to breach or circumvent the technology. She additionally insists that legal sanctions will, one imagines, not stop those who either do not care or who are not afraid of consequences. Johnson places her faith in ethical commitment.

The inculcation of positive values that subsequently guide and control an individual's activity is preferable to technology and the law, but it is inadequate. Only those who choose to avoid doing wrong, only those who opt to cooperate, will act in a socially and ethically tenable manner. The unprincipled or fearless who prefer asocial, unethical activity will crack, steal, and harm. Obviously technological devices, legal sanctions, and ethical mandates working in tandem with each other provide the best solution available for controlling ourselves as well as information seekers in a society in which data, information, and knowledge have greater intrinsic value than any other commodity.

Concluding Remarks

Ethics matters because it helps us to act responsibly. A stubborn adherence to organizational rules or even to the law is an easy but not necessarily correct way to solve complex problems; a true commitment to ethical decision making produces traumatic dilemmas. The person who thinks things through and makes a decision based on the evidence in light of what he or she believes to be correct, is acting ethically. When two opposing principles vie with each other, it is much easier to capitulate to necessity. The Florida librarian, who discovered that some of the terrorists responsible for the destruction of the World Trade Center had used networked computers, acted in a socially responsible way by contacting the police. We hold that confientiality is unbreachable but concomitantly, most people believe that the protection of life should receive the highest priority. Some commentators insist that professional librarians must wait for a subpoena to arrive before offering to help the authorities and even then some may balk. (In the Florida case, the police were unaware of the situation.) I insist that in extreme exigencies, one has a higher duty to society to protect people and property. I wonder whether those who advocate non-cooperation would withhold information if they knew that their actions would cost the lives of their loved ones. This is certainly a very difficult case, and the decision one makes will be based on the principles that he or she favors. I dislike calling upon the law in orer to convince information workers that professional rules and regulations are sometimes misguided or expungeable, but nevertheless I note that the *USA Patriot Act* alters the way in which we must respond to a warrant. This is not necessarily a positive development, since it allows the government to carry out secret investigations and disempowers people who may not discuss what has occurred. These are hard and dangerous times. For a quarter of a century, I have maintained that social necessity outweighs professional obligations. I continue to insist that this is the case. Generally, it is possible to fulfill professional mandates without concomitantly sacrificing civil liberties. We do this by making considered and judicious choices.

Lest readers accuse me of pessimistic negativism, of perceiving and affirming the problems and disparities in information access and dissemination, to the exclusion of all that is good, meaningful, and useful, I would note that this is a study of ethical procedures and challenges, and the substantive matter entails a concentration on negativities. If the path to be followed were clear, then ethical considerations would be superfluous and *Ethics and Librarianship* would have remained unwritten. There are good and competent people in librarianship and they often do what they should. This volume can help them succeed more often.

I have concentrated on analytic and descriptive methods. Those readers who would have preferred less analysis, fewer opinions, and more situational challenges can satisfy this craving by consulting Herbert White's (1992) *Ethical Dilemmas in Libraries* and Fay Zipkowitz's (1996) *Professional Ethics in Librarianship,* two collections of useful case studies.

Bibliography

Abandoning the comfort zone: Making medical reference accountable. (1994, September). *American Libraries 25* (8), 772ff. Retrieved February 5, 2001, from *Infotrac* database (EAI) on the World Wide Web: http://web7.infotrac.galegroup.com/itw/session/

Albanese, A. (2001, March 1). AAP's Schroeder impugns Libns., ILL. *Library Journal*, 12–13.

Alfino, M., and Pierce, L. (1997). *Information ethics for librarians.* Jefferson, NC: McFarland.

_____, and _____. (2001, Winter). The social nature of information. *Library Trends 49* (3), 471–485.

Altman, E., & Hernon, P. (Eds.). (1997). *Research misconduct: Issues, implications, and strategies.* Greenwich, CT: Ablex.

Angoff, A. (1976, September). Library malpractice suit: Could it happen to you? *American Libraries 7,* 489.

Asheim, L. (1953, September). Not censorship but selection. *Wilson Library Bulletin,* 63–67.

Berman, S. (1971). *Prejudices and antipathies: A tract on the LC subject heads concerning people.* Metuchen, NJ: Scarecrow.

_____. (1988). Where have all the moonies gone? In *Worth noting: Editorials, letters, essays, an interview, and bibliography* (pp. 23–31). Jefferson, NC: McFarland.

Bielefield, A., & Cheeseman, L. (1993). *Libraries & Copyright Law.* New York: Neal-Schuman.

Board of Education, Island Trees Union Free School District No. 26 v. Pico, 102 S. Ct. 2799 (1982).

Boissonnas, C. M. (1987). The cost is more than that elegant dinner: Your ethics are at steak. *Library Acquisitions: Practice & Theory 11*, 145–152.

Bornstein. J. (1999). Ethical conflicts confronted by librarians in news media. *Journal of Mass Media Ethics 14* (3), 159–170.

Bradsher, K. (2000, Februray 24). Town rejects bid to curb library's Internet access. *The New York Times*, p. A12.

Branscomb, A. W. (1994). *Who owns information? From privacy to public access.* New York: Basic Books.

Bridis, T., and Simpson, G. R. (2001, June 20). Many federal agencies may fail to comply with law helping disabled access web. *The Wall Street Journal*, p. B2.

Bruwelheide, J. H. (1995). *The copyright primer for librarians and educators.* (2nd ed). Chicago: American Library Association and Washington, DC: National Education Association.

Buesseler, C., et al. (1999). Pragamatic capitulation: Why the information specialist censors. *Library Talk, 12* (3), 20–21.

Burke, M., et al. (1996, Summer). Editorial: Fraud and misconduct in library and information science research. *Library and Information Science Research, 18*, 199–206.

Burt, D. (1997, August). In defense of filtering. *American Libraries*, 46, 48.

Bushing, M. C. (1993). Acquisition ethics: The evolution of models for hard times. *Library Acquisitions: Practice & Theory 17*, 47–52.

Byrne, P. (2001, January 5). Constitutional academic freedom in scholarship and in court. *The Chronicle of Higher Education*, p. B13.

Capurro, R. (1988). Informationsethos und informationsethik.... *Nachrichten für Dokumentation, 39* (1), 1–4.

Chilton, B. S. (1993, Fall). Managing information services in the public interest ethic. *Journal of Information Ethics 2* (2), 44–52.

Christianson, M. (2001, February). The irate patron is right. *College & Research Libraries News*, 189–191.

Cohen, A. (2001, July 2). Internet insecurity. *Time*, pp. 44–51.

Crawford, H. (1978, July). In search of an ethic of medical librarianship. *Bulletin of the Medical Library Association 66*, (3), 331–337.

Crews, K. D. (1990). Copyright policies at American research universities: Balancing information needs and legal limits. Los Angeles: University of California. Unpublished dissertation.

Cronin, Blaise. (2000, September 1). Whatever happened to common sense? *Library Journal* , 177.

Danielson, E. S. (1997). Ethics and reference services. *The Reference Librarian 56*, 107–124.

Database of Editors. (2000). Editors of 100 of the highest-priced journal titles. Retrieved January 19, 2001, from the World Wide Web: http://www.arl.org/create/resources/journal.html

Dick, A. L. (1995, April). Library and information science as a social science: Neutral and normative conceptions. *Library Quarterly 65* (2), 216–235.

Dickens, C. (1996). *Bleak House*. London, Oxford.

Elias, S. (1999). *Patent, copyright & trademark*. 3rd ed. Berkeley, CA: Nolo Press.

Ewing, K., & Hauptman, R. (1995, January). Is traditional reference service obsolete? *The Journal of Academic Librarianship, 21* (1), 3–6.

Ferguson, S. & Weckert, J. (1998, October). The librarian's duty of care: Emerging professionalism or can of worms. *Library Quarterly.* Retrieved from *Infotrac* database (EAI) on the World Wide Web: http://Web7.infotrac.galegroup.com/itw/session/

Fish, S. (1985). Antiprofessionalism. *New Literary History, 17* (1), 89–107.

Flagg, G. (2001, April). Legislation announced to protect fair use. *American Libraries, 32* (4), 16. Accessed on June 25, 2001, from InfoTrac OneFile http://web7.infotrac.galegroup.com/itw/i

Foskett, D. J. (1962). *The creed of a librarian: No politics, no religion, no morals.* London: Library Association.

Foster, A. L. (2001, January 19). Supreme Court rebuffs professors' challenge to a Virginia law on Internet use. *The Chronicle of Higher Education,* p. A31.

_____. (2001, June 1). Bill would ease some copyright restrictions. *The Chronicle of Higher Education,* p. A30.

Frazier, K. (1999). Collection development and professional ethics. *Journal of Library Administration, 28* (1), 33–46.

Freeman, D. (1999). *The fateful hoaxing of Margaret Mead: A historical analysis of her Samoan research.* Boulder: Westview.

Fricke, M., Mathiesen, K., & Fallis, D. (2000, October). The ethical presuppositions behind the Library Bill of Rights. *Library Quarterly 70* (4), 468ff. Retrieved February 16, 2001, from *Infotrac* database (EAI) on the World Wide Web: http://web7.infotrac.galegroup.com/itw/session/

Froehlich, T. J. (1992). Ethical issues in the consultant-library relationship. In E. D. Garten (Ed.), *Using consultants in libraries and information centers (pp. 155–172).* Westport, CT: Greenwood.

_____. (1997). Survey and analysis of the major ethical and legal issues facing library and information services. IFLA Publications 78. München: K. G. Saur.

Frohmann, B. (2000, September/December). Cyber ethics: Bodies or bytes? *The International Information and Library Review 32* (3–4), 423–435.

Gann, R. (1995, June). The therapeutic partnership: Legal and ethical aspects of consumer health information. *Health Libraries Review 12* (2), 83–90.

Gasaway, L. N., & Wiant, S K. (1994). *Libraries and copyright: A guide to copyright law in the 1990s.* Washington, DC: Special Libraries Association.

Geer, B. (1995, Fall). Unusual citings: Journal citation integrity and the public services librarian. *RQ 35* (1), 67–73.

Gleick, E. (1995, September 25). She spoke volumes. *Time,* 52.

Gorman, M. (2000). *Our Enduring Values: Librarianship in the 21st century.* Chicago: American Library Association.

Grafton, A. (1997). *The footnote: A curious history.* Cambridge, MA: Harvard.

Green, J. (1990). *The encyclopedia of censorship.* New York: Facts on File.

Greenhouse, L. (2001, June 26). Freelancers win in copyright case. *The New York Times,* pp. A1, A14.

Gremmels, G. S. (1991, Spring). Reference in the public interest: An examination of ethics. *RQ, 30* (3), 362–369.

Guernsey, L. (1998, July 31). Off-Campus users swamp college libraries, seeking access to Web and e-mail. *The Chronicle of Higher Education,* pp. A17, A19.

Hamilton, R. F. (1996). *The Social Misconstruction of Reality.* New Haven: Yale.

Hannabuss, S. (in press). *Information liability and negligence.* London: Library Association.

Hannigan, J. A., & Crew, H. (1993, October). A feminist paradigm for library and information science. *Wilson Library Bulletin,* 28–32.

Harer, J. B. (1992). *Intellectual freedom: A reference handbook.* Santa Barbara, CA: ABC-CLIO.

Hauptman, R. (1976, April). Professionalism or culpability: An experiment in ethics. *Wilson Library Bulletin, 50* (8), 626–627.

_____. (1988). *Ethical challenges in librarianship.* Phoenix: Oryx.

_____. (ed.). (1992–). *Journal of Information Ethics.*

_____. (1999, October). Bibliographic essay: Information ethics. *Choice, 37* (2), 261–273.

Hernon, P., and Altman, E. (1995, January). Misconduct in academic research…. *The Journal of Academic Librarianship 21* (1), 27–37.

_____, and _____. (1999, September). Misconduct: Infecting the literature, but do we *really* care? *The Journal of Academic Librarianship 25* (5), 402–404.

_____, & McClure, C. R. (1986, April 15). Unobtrusive reference testing: The 55 percent rule. *Library Journal,* 37ff.

Hitchcock, L. A. (2000). Perspectives on … Enriching the record. *The Journal of Academic Librarianship, 26* (5), 359–363.

http://v.hbi-stuttgart.de/~capurro/icie-index.html

http://www.sis.pitt.edu/~ethics

Intner, S. S. (1993, November). Ethics in cataloging. *Technicalities 13* (11), 5–8.

Irish, D. E. (1992, November). And ne'er the twain shall meet? Personal vs. professional ethics. *The Christian Librarian,* 36 (1), 14–19.

Johnson, D. G. (1997, January). Ethics online. *Commmunications of the ACM, 40* (1), 60–65.

Jones, B. M. (1999). *Libraries, access, and intellectual freedom: Developing policies for public and academic libraries.* Chicago: American Library Association.

Kafka, F. (1984). *The Trial.* New York: Schocken Books.

Kant, I. (1949). *Fundamental principles of the metaphysics of morals.* Indianapolis: Bobbs-Merrill.

Kingsley, M. S., and Berwick, P. C. (1990). Plain English for publishers: An articulation of billing problems. In K. Strauch and B. Strauch (Eds.), *Legal and ethical issues in acquisitions* (pp. 27–36). New York: Haworth.

Kirkpatrick, D. D. (2000, December 25). Librarians unite against cost of journals. *The New York Times,* p. C5.

Kornblum, J. (2000, May 8). Porn makes workplace hostile, 7 librarians say. *USA Today,* p. 3D.

Lewis, M. (2001, July 15). Faking it. *The New York Times Magazine*, pp. 32–37, 44, 61–63.

Library of Congress cited for fire risks. (2001, March 6). *The New York Times*, p. A13.

Library sued for not censoring Web porn. (1999, January 4). *USA Today*, p. 6A.

Lorenzo, P. (1995, Spring/Fall). Answering legal questions at the reference desk: Issues of ethics, liability, and use of legal collections. *Current Studies in Librarianship 19* (1, 2), 13–23.

Machlup, F. (1962). *The production and distribution of knowledge in the United States*. Princeton, NJ: Princeton.

MacNeil, H. (1992). *Without consent: The ethics of disclosing personal information in public archives*. np: Society of American Archivists; Metuchen, NJ: Scarecrow.

Mainstream Loudoun v. Board of Trustees of the Loudoun County Library, 24 F. Supp. 2d 552 (1998).

Manning, A. (2001, July 9). Poor countries will get medical journal access. *USA Today*, p. 7D.

Marco, G. A. (1996, March). Ethics for librarians: A narrow view. *Journal of Librarianship and Information Science 28* (1), 33–38.

Marcum, D. (1997). A moral and legal obligation: Preservation in the digital age. *The International Information & Library Review, 29*, 357–365.

Martin, S. (1997, March 14). Federal panel seeks to end 'culture of secrecy' that restricts historical records. *The Chronicle of Higher Education*, p. A28.

Martin, S. K. (1999, May). When vision encounters reality: A professional dilemma.*The Journal of Academic Librarianship, 25* (3), 223.

Mazikana, P. (1997). The challenges of archiving digital information. The *International Information & Library Review 29*, 307–317.

McCook, K. D. L. P. (Ed.). (2000). *Library Trends 49* (1), entire issue.

McDonald, F. B. (1993). *Censorship and intellectual freedom: A survey of school librarians' attitudes and moral reasoning*. Metuchen, NJ: Scarecrow.

McDowell, B. (2000). *Ethics and excuses: The crisis in professional responsibility*. Westport, CT: Quorum.

Merton, R. K. (1973). The normative structure of science. In his *The sociology of science* (pp. 267–278). Chicago: University of Chicago. (Original work published 1942, 1985, September 15).

Mintz, A.P. (1985, September 15). Information practice and malpractice. *Library Journal*, 38–43.

Mitroff, I. (1974). *The Subjective Side of Science*. New York: Elsevier.

Moran, G. (1998). Silencing scientists and scholars in other fields: Power, paradigm controls, peer review, and scholarly communication. Greenwich, CT: Ablex.

Nesta, F. & Blanke, H. (1991, May 15). Warning: Propaganda. *Library Journal*, 41–43.

Office for Intellectual Freedom. (Comp.). (1996). *Intellectual freedom manual*. (5th ed.). Chicago: American Library Association.

Olson, H. A. (2001). The power to name: Representation in library catalogs. *Signs, 26* (3), 639–668.

Orlans, H. (1998, November-December). Information costs challenged. *Change 30* (6), 7. Retrieved January 15, 2001, from *Infotrac* database (EAI) on the World

Wide Web: http://web7.infotrac.galegroup.com/itw/session/

Page, G. (1990.) Money, means and content. *The Serials Librarian, 17* (3–4),1–13.

Patry, W. F. (1985). *The Fair Use Privilege in copyright law.* Washington, DC: The Bureau of National Affairs.

Patterson, L. R., & Lindberg, S. W. (1991). *The nature of copyright: A law of users' rights.* Athens, GA: University of Georgia.

Peck, R. S. (1996). School library censorship and the courts: After Hazelwood. In Office for Intellectual Freedom (comp.), *Intellectual freedom manual.* (5th ed.) (pp. 311–322). Chicago: American Library Association.

Pendergrast, M. (1988, June 1). In praise of labeling or, when shalt thou break commandments? *Library Journal,* 83–85.

Piternick, A. B. (1989, November). Attempts to find alternatives to the scientific journal: A brief review. *The Journal of Academic Librarianship 15* (5), 260–266.

Preer, J. (1991, Winter). Special ethics for special librarians? *Special Libraries,* 12–18.

Protti, M. E. (1991, Fall). Dispensing law at the front lines: Ethical dilemmas in law librarianship. *Library Trends 40* (2), 234–243.

Puckett, M., & Craig, J. P. (1993). Information malpractice. In A. Kent (Ed.), `*Encyclopedia of library and information science* (Vol. 52, Supplement 15, pp. 141–167). New York: Marcel Dekker.

Rainey, N. B. (1988). Ethical principles and liability risks in providing drug information. *Medical Reference Services Quarterly, 7* (3), 59–67.

Rogers, W. G. (1965). *Wise men fish here: The story of Frances Steloff and the Gotham Book Mart.* New York: Harcourt, Brace & World.

Rouse, V. (1999, June). Making the WEB accessible. *Computers in Libraries 19* (6), 48ff. Retrieved February 5, 2001, from *Infotrac* database (EAI) on the World Wide Web: http://web7.infotrac.galegroup.com/itw/session/

Rubin, R. R., & Froehlich, T. J. (1996). Ethical aspects of library and information science. In A. Kent (Ed.), *Encyclopedia of Library and Information Science* (Vol. 58, Supplement 21, pp. 33–52). New York: Marcel Dekker.

Rude, R. & Hauptman, R. (1993). Theft, dissimulation and trespass: Some observations on security. *Library & Archival Security, 12* (1), 17–22.

Rudolph, J., & Brackstone, D. (1990, April 11). Too many scholars ignore the basic rules of documentation. *The Chronicle of Higher Education,* p. A56.

RUSA guidelines. (2000, Winter). *Reference & User Services Quarterly 40* (2), 118–119.

St. Clair, G. (1997). *Total quality management in information services.* London: Bowker-Saur.

Samuelson, P. (1993, January). Liability for defective electronic information. *Communications of the ACM, 36* (1), 21–26.

Sandstrom, A. R. and Sandstrom, P. E. (1995, April). The use and misuse of anthropological methods in library and information science research. *The Library Quarterly 65* (2), 161–199.

Sanger, D. E. (2001, January 17). Report on Holocaust assets tells of items found in U.S. *The New York Times,* p. A12.

Schanck, P. C. (1999, June). Avoiding conflicts of interest in vendor-librarian transactions. *The Law Librarian 31* (2), 131–134.

Schwartz, J. (2000, December 21). Protests arise over business aspect of censoring web. *The New York Times*, p. C4.

Schweinsburg, J.D. (1995, Fall). Professional awareness of the ethics of selection. *Journal of Information Ethics, 4* (2), 33–42.

Severson, R. (1995, Spring). The recovery of ethics in librarianship. *Journal of Information Ethics, 4* (1), 11–16.

Severson, R. J. (1997). *The principles of information ethics.* Armonk, NY: M. E. Sharpe.

Smith, M. (2001, Winter). Global information justice: Rights, responsibilities, and caring connections. *Library Trends 49* (3), 519–537.

Smith, M. M. (1998). Information ethics. In M. C. Williams, ed. *Annual review of Information science and technology, 32* (1997) (pp. 339–366). Medford, NJ: Information Today.

Stille, A. (2001, June 2). Adding up the costs of cyberdemocracy. *The New York Times*, pp. B9, B11.

Swan, J. C. (1998). Untruth or consequences? In R. N. Stichler and R. Hauptman (Eds.), *Ethics, information, and technology: Readings* (pp. 64–75). Jefferson, NC: McFarland.

Taylor, J. K. (1997, Fall). Protecting minors from free speech. *Journal of Information Ethics, 6* (2), 67–74.

third-graders defend Harry Potter. (2000, March). *Newsletter on Intellectual Freedom*, 46.

Tierney, P. (2000). *Darkness in El Dorado.* New York: Norton.

Trosow, S. E. (2001, January). When is a use a fair use? University liability for educational copying. *portal: libraries and the academy, 1* (1), 47–57.

van Tonder, S. (1994). Kommunikasie in die gesondheidsorgmilieu: Voorsiening en weerhouding van inligting. *Mousaion 12* (1), 21–33.

Wan, R. (1994, November/December). Reflections on malpractice of reference librarians. *Public Libraries, 33*, 305–309.

Werner, G. S. (2000, March). SPARC — alternatives to high-cost journals. *American Libraries*, 52.

Westwood, K. (1994, February). Prison law librarianship: A lesson in service for all librarians. *American Libraries, 25* (2), 152ff. Retrieved February 17, 2001, from *Infotrac* database (EAI) on the World Wide Web: http://web7.infotrac. galegroup.com/itw/session/

White, H. S. (1992). *Ethical dilemmas in libraries: A collection of case studies.* New York: G. K. Hall.

Wiener, P. B. (1987, January/February). On my mind: Mad bombers and ethical librarians: A dialogue with Robert Hauptman and John Swan. *Catholic Library World, 58* (4), 161–163.

Wilson, E. O. (1975). *Sociobiology: The new synthesis.* Cambridge, MA: Harvard.

Winkler, K. J. (1983, May 25). Publishers vs. librarians: Economic woes pit former allies against one another. *The Chronicle of Higher Education*, pp. 29, 31.

Wood, M. S. (1991, Fall). Public service ethics in health sciences libraries. *Library Trends 40* (2), 244–257.

Zipkowitz, F. (1996). *Professional ethics in librarianship: A real life casebook.*

Index